D1592877

Truth and Existence

Truth
and
Existence

A Philosophical Inquiry

Michael Gelven

The Pennsylvania State University Press
University Park and London

The quotation from "Words," copyright © 1960 by W. H. Auden, is reprinted from *W. H. Auden: Collected Poems,* edited by Edward Mendelson, by permission of Random House, Inc.

Library of Congress Cataloging-in-Publication Data

Gelven, Michael.
    Truth and existence: a philosophical inquiry / Michael Gelven.

        p.   cm.
    ISBN 0-271-00707-9 (alk. paper)
    1. Truth.   I. Title.
BD161.G45   1990
121—dc20   90–31683

It is the policy of The Pennsylvania State University Press to use acid-free paper for the first printing of all clothbound books. Publications on uncoated stock satisfy the minimum requirements of American National Standard for Information Sciences— Permanence of Paper for Printed Library Materials, ANSI Z39.48–1984.

To Annette Mumma and Tom Schall

Contents

Acknowledgments

Because truth must be acknowledged and acknowledgment often entails gratitude, I recognize a joyous indebtedness to Herman Stark, friend and critic, who in sundry ways helped make this singular inquiry exciting, honest, and possible.

Permission to quote from the poem "Words" by W. H. Auden is kindly granted by Random House, Inc., New York; the British permissions have been granted by Faber and Faber, London.

The four lines from Nono's poem in Tennessee William's *Night of the Iguana*, © 1961 by Two Rivers Enterprises, Inc., are reprinted by permission of New Directions Publishing Corp., New York.

PART ONE
RAISING THE PROBLEM

1

The Worth of Truth

Throughout our literary and philosophical heritage, Truth has been prized as among the loftiest of notions, deserving our reverence and devotion. We are assured by Christian letters that the truth shall make us free; Socrates is considered an honored martyr for truth; medieval theologians rank it along with the Good and the One among the great triad of transcendentals. Opposing systems, ideologies, theologies, and faiths all claim truth as their own. Since we seem to have a good number of facts which are not particularly interesting or even worthy of being known, apparently such reverence is not accorded to truths in the plural—that is, things which we know—but to Truth with an initial capital and always in the singular. Why this Truth should make us free, or why someone dying for it should evoke our admiration, is not completely clear, though the notion is surely appealing. Nor is just what Truth means indisputably obvious, but there can be no doubt that it is honored, even if its meaning is vague.

Poets rank truth as equal to their own totem, beauty. Tolstoy writes that there is only one fair and radiant hero in all his works, the beloved figure Truth. Keats tells us that "truth is beauty, and beauty truth"; and Emily Dickinson entombs the pair in a common crypt:

> I died for beauty—but was scarce
> Adjusted in the tomb
> When one who died for Truth
> Was lain in an adjoining room.

With such prestigious and lofty endorsements, surely this notion, truth, deserves our interest and attention. But why is truth so highly rated? What, after all, is the worth of truth?

On the one hand nothing seems so common as truth. Everyone says hundreds of true sentences everyday, and even in speculative cases where our knowledge is uncertain, disjunctive thinking guarantees truth in at least fifty percent of the claims; for either God exists or he does not, and my ignorance of which does not keep one of these metaphysical assertions from being true. It would seem anything that ubiquitous, that available, that ordinary should not be praised so highly as Christ, Socrates, Keats, and Tolstoy seem to praise truth. On the other hand, when we speak of truth in the reverential way that these four men have done it seems we do not mean what can be found so plentifully in our daily sentences. "Paris is south of London" is true, but its being true will not make us free, nor will it ennoble the death of Socrates or ever deserve to be equated with beauty, nor does it belong with the One and the Good. And so it seems that rather than being a surfeit, truth is a rarity. When we speak of truth in the noble sense (whatever that may mean) we seem to think of it as some distant but majestic source of great illumination or tranquillity, perhaps forever out of reach to mere mortals, beckoning as the sirens do to the promise of the spectacular and wonderful. Or, in a counterintuition, truth seems to lurk deeply within the fundamental darkness of things, requiring great penetration or digging to discover. In the first image truth is a distant sun, the glimpse of which can only be achieved by mounting the highest peak; in the second it is a piece of gold buried in the deepest rock, attainable only by the herculean efforts of a miner. But with either picture, for miner or mountaineer, truth is that which is finally unattainable in its fullness, though glimpses of it can be achieved by great efforts.

Is truth then available to us as wantonly as a common sentence? Or is it unavailable to us in its lofty distance? If it is the first, its very commonness makes it cheap by being so plentiful; if it is the second, its very distance seems to make it irrelevant to most of us, so why bother with it? It is either so near that it becomes trivial, or so very far out of our sight that it is also out of mind. In either case, what is its worth? If it is lofty it certainly cannot be discoverable by the analysis of mere sentences; and if it is so rare, perhaps it cannot be discovered at all. Therefore, as Falstaff says of honor, "I'll none of it."

But these reflections are absurd. Of course truth is important. Examples as ample as the day itself emerge in our thought with the scarcest bidding. The importance of truth? Why, just consider a few random samples. We demand that our witnesses take an oath to tell the truth, and only the truth, to ensure we achieve justice. We pay our biological scientists great sums for searching into the viral jungles to get at truth so we can cure our diseases. We instruct our young to tell the truth so they will be seen as having good characters. These are but three advantages to truth, and even if we restrict ourselves to these, surely they suffice to make truth an obvious treasure.

There is no doubt we use truth to achieve these great boons. But that is precisely the point. We *use* truth because we want something else. Truth then becomes a means and not an end in itself. By demanding that our witnesses tell the truth to ensure justice, we imply that it is not truth but justice that is of worth. The truths of science may prove beneficial to our health, so it is health that is important, not truth. Our children tell the truth so they will be honored as having good character, so it is honor that matters, not truth. But whatever is a means to another end is of lesser rank than what it serves. To borrow from an older vocabulary, granted truth has extrinsic worth, does it have any intrinsic worth? That is, can we venerate truth just by itself? Perhaps the truth is that truth has no rank at all.

To confuse what has mere instrumental value with something of intrinsic worth is not only a conceptual error, it is a moral mistake deserving censure. We call a man a miser who has forgotten that money is valuable because of what it can buy. A miser treats money as a thing of worth in itself, like one's child or spouse, something to be loved. But miserliness is known as a vice, and the miser is looked down upon with contempt and pity. If truth, like money, is valuable only insofar as it can bring us more precious things, then to rank it as something precious in and of itself is both a conceptual error and a moral mistake. It is a vice, like being a miser. This vice is known as philosophy, and to deprecate truth from intrinsic to extrinsic value is to forfeit the status of this already maligned and dubious discipline. If the philosopher loves truth for its own sake, and if the truth is that truth has no sake of its own, then philosophy is a vice and the philosopher both a miscreant and a fool. Fools mistake the journey for the destination; they rank the hoe and rake above the flowering garden, and the worker's toil above his wage. Not wishing to be foolish, for a fool affronts both thought and goodness, we must take seriously these attacks which demote truth to a servile role, for otherwise we become idolators rather than true worshipers, confusing the icon with the god.

It is imperative to consider the opposite side of the question. Is not truth often undesirable? There are some truths that are so horrible we shun them, and would not consider knowing them a benefit at all. We hesitate to tell a vulnerable child the true wickedness of his mother lest it destroy him. Perhaps we are glad we do not know when we are going to die. Were there some deep malignancy eroding the number of our days, would it not be better to live them in blissful ignorance? And indeed, if one could achieve justice by telling a lie, would not one dissemble? It is not difficult to imagine such a case. Both truth and untruth then can serve justice; so why rank the one above the other?

Or let us consider the poignancy of Dickinson's poem. There are those, we say, who die for the truth. But there are also those who die for what they believe. Beliefs are not always true. Yet we honor those who die for their beliefs even if those beliefs are false. In honoring Socrates as a martyr for truth are we not really merely saying he died for his beliefs? What is the difference between dying for the truth and dying for one's beliefs? To be sure, the martyr may believe his false beliefs are true, but his cognitive mistake in no way lessens our admiration for his courage or his loyalty to what he believes. Hence it would seem we do not honor those who die for truth; we merely honor those millions of dedicated, finite people who are willing to sacrifice their lives for what they believe. And this is the cruel irony, that the Platonic preference for truth over belief here is curiously inverted: we honor the believer, and not the truth. So truth, as truth, does not seem to matter at all.

An imagined consideration along these lines may be helpful. Let us assume a theological-metaphysical system which provides for its believers greater happiness, pleasure, well-being, and moral strength than are available to any nonbeliever; let us also assume that any believer in this system will in fact not suffer any post-terrestrial punishment for his belief. Finally let us assume this system is false. But if *believing* in this system brings all possible benefits and no danger of post-terrestrial punishment, why should the falseness of it matter at all? And if it seems that the falseness cannot matter—and we have built this indifference into the assumption—then surely it cannot matter whether such a system is true. Believing in such systems would then matter enormously, but their truth or falsity would matter not at all. It would seem then that opinion or belief truly is superior to truth, for it is easy to find examples in which different opinions matter, and seemingly impossible to find cases where truth makes any difference whatsoever.

Indeed, the greatest achievements of mankind surely are those which have nothing to do with truth and much to do with untruth. Not one philosophical treatise published in the last fifty years equals a single mature play by Shakespeare; and all the lives of an entire university faculty are not as influential as one day in the life of the mature Julius Caesar, and Caesar worshiped power, not truth. Surely it is Lenin and not Marx who has more influenced the world. And Shakespeare's plays are not only untrue, they positively celebrate illusion. "The truest poetry is the most feigning," Touchstone says in *As You Like It;* and audiences are willing to be persuaded of the lie that fools triumph in love or that the death of Lear is somehow glorious. But it is not glorious, it is gruesome. What is glorious is the fame, the achievement, the sheer irrational majesty of deception. Before these mighty triumphs of the false, meek and irrelevant truth can only wonder and crawl away in shame. By almost any standard, the false, the feigning, the deceptive, the prevaricators, the dissemblers, the counterfeits, the liars, the disguisers, the beguilers, and the tricksters rank far and away more successful and worthy than the true. Indeed, the very words which indicate the false far outnumber the apparently single and lonely word we have for the opposing notion. It is perhaps the only word in the language with no synonym. (There are some pale candidates, like 'accurate' and 'genuine,' but they do not equal the elusive power of 'truth'.) The false has a thousand lovely names, suggesting the infinite variety and richness it offers, but the true names only itself. The false is diverse and distracting, the truth is neither. The false brings endless sources of pleasure, entertainment, joy, and narcotic distraction, the true brings nothing but its sober self. How then to justify this curious ranking that seems to be given to truth in spite of its obvious impoverishment?

Perhaps the worth of truth has been misprized by those who pretend to honor it. And this we can uneasily suspect, that the very praise of truth given by those master dissemblers like Keats and Dickinson is, at bottom, just another lie. A lie, told perhaps to trick us into accepting briefly what we could never really accept. So that the very honor given truth serves its opponent in the end. The false is honored by the false praise of the true.

But if these great writers have indeed deceived us, what would it matter if truth does not? Why should such deception, if it is deception, disturb us at all? If truth is of value merely in helping us achieve other important things like justice and health, then this false praise of the true is of no serious concern, and we may take the whole matter with fleeting indifference or even delight. For what harm is done if truth is devalued like the coinage of a deposed regime? The loss of prestige is no great loss, for if one cannot show the hurt in the loss, there is no pleasure in the gain. What harm of any sort can come from the debasement of so impecunious an exchequer as the pocketless urchin, the boy truth, who like love is perjured everywhere?

It may be fitting to put a bullet in the brain of this impoverished wretch. Has truth even extrinsic worth? The truth we expect to serve us in our search for justice is really only honesty. We demand that our witnesses be honest, not truthful. And the so-called truth we expect from our scientists is really only adherence to the canons of objectivity. For it is the results we want, and honesty and objectivity may help us get them, but truth provides nothing in their behalf. Perhaps, indeed, truth is not only worthless and useless but also meaningless. Perhaps, that is, truth not only lacks intrinsic value (it is worthless) and extrinsic value (it is useless), but is a mere usurpatory notion, which adds nothing when it is present and detracts nothing when it is absent (it is meaningless).

To see that truth is meaningless, consider the following sentences:

1. All men suffer.
2. It is true all men suffer.

Does the second sentence add anything not already contained in the first sentence? It seems not. Hence the expression 'it is true' adds nothing. It is a mere stylistic device which intensifies what is said. But if truth adds nothing but stylistic embellishment, it is a usurpatory concept like luck or fate; it is appealed to as if it explained, but in fact it does not.

If truth is a usurpatory concept, then it in no way deserves the praises heaped upon it by the great writers; indeed it deserves rather to be maligned. Far from being equated with goodness and beauty, it should be defiled as loathsome, for not only is it worthless, as a usurper it should be quarantined as a noisome pestilence. But the quarantine of truth seems to be precisely what has occurred in our contemporary culture, especially in education. Western thinkers, particularly Americans, are taught from infancy that there is no truth at all; there is only opinion, or value, or one system versus another system, one epoch following another. We beatify tolerance to the point where any claim of truth is seen as positively un-American. Parents refuse to pass on a tradition lest the result be seen as a kind of brainwashing. From the proliferation of religious cults to the violent demonstrations in the streets, from the obscene polling of the political spectrum to the savage tyranny of the new over the refined in art, this culture is intoxicated with the brew of relativism, until we are reeling down our streets, giggling and blinded by the liquor of indifference to truth. It has indeed been quarantined, for its contagion threatens to make what is unchanging and unconditioned matter.

Truth has become 'true for me', which of course does not make any sense. The search for truth is supplanted by a find of isms and ideologies. To believe in truth is seen as a regression to. bigotry, whereas our greatest achievements are seen as anything which merely challenges traditional values, regardless of whether the challenges are true. But this erosion of truth and the respect for truth has occurred not only in the public market and on the populist airwaves, but in the very hallowed halls of the philosophical institutions themselves. How can truth be honored if those whose business it is to uncover the truth have been exiled from their proper home? A brief analysis of two recent academic assaults on the integrity of truth may show how this is happening. The first of these, perhaps now passé, interprets philosophers in terms of their psyche rather than their thought. This turns our attention to the soundness of a thinker's mind rather than his ideas; the health of the psyche has replaced the truth of the inquiry. We are asked to consider great philosophical works as the offspring of unhealthy and suppressed libidos. In such clinical sterility the life of truth cannot survive, for the philosopher does not care why a thinker writes what he does, but merely whether what he has written is true.

A second, perhaps more sinister and certainly more prevalent quarantine of truth occurs when we are asked to read all the great ideas as mere causes and effects in the vast influentialist account of what is known as intellectual history, in which an idea is judged not by its truth but by its pedigree. No one denies that thinkers are influenced by their predecessors, and that their own thinking influences their posterity, but the point of their inquiry is not merely to be pinned on the historical chart like specimens, but to be weighed as possible candidates for truth. But truth is once again made irrelevant by the intellectual historian, for whom the sole source of enlightenment from the great ideas is the role they play in the emerging history of an intellectual movement. Truth has become a mere plaything in the hands of uncaring academicians who see it as a source for the links that bind the mindless and purposeless events of conceptual history into an amusing and entertaining story of no more worth or authority than a fable.

And thus truth is no longer a mere servant of other goods, or even a beggar, but a corpse regarded by a few solemn nostalgists as a figure who may once have lived but is now only remembered. It lies in state and is mourned perhaps, but no longer regarded as important or authoritative. If the psychoanalysts debase truth by rendering ideas a form of sexual gratification, intellectual historians entomb it and perform funeral services over the mound. For never do these contemporary critics ask the one question which all the thinkers themselves thought alone mattered: "Yes, but is it *true?*" This question is no longer asked for the simple reason that no one knows what it *means.* It is not modern to ask it.

Perhaps, however, this obituary is somewhat premature. It is not, after all, only pre-twentieth-century figures who praise truth; so do W. H. Auden and Iris Murdoch and Martin Heidegger, all contemporaries. Furthermore, many of the dismissals of truth in the above indictments are misleading. For to die for truth remains a totally different kind of sacrifice than to die for one's beliefs. Socrates was put to death not because of his beliefs but because of his inquiries and because he championed the notion of truth against the notion of persuasion, even though he admitted his own ignorance. Furthermore, the protest that the phrase 'it is true' adds nothing to the claim 'all men die' is wrong; on the highest level these three words make all the difference in the world. And though there may be too many troops among the armies of intellectual historians and psychoanalytic interpreters, the truth-seekers have always been here, like partisans in a dark forest, waiting for a chance to repel the alien invaders. The morticians who would bury truth must first find it, and that is a more demanding task than they, with their meager resources, are equal to.

It is true that a miser who takes money for an end and not for a mere means is a fool. But those who speak so glowingly of truth are not fools, for the confusion of means and ends does not apply to the wise. When they speak so nobly of truth, there is authority in what they say. It is the authority of truth itself. Truth matters uniquely. It fails in all tests of analogy, as we have seen in the preceding sections, precisely because it is disanalogous to all other notions. It is bootless to seek for the benefits of truth or for the advantages of truth, since what one seeks is none of these but the truth of truth. Nevertheless, this abortive attempt to discover the worth of truth is deeply troubling. By trying to praise truth we find there is no readily available support for doing so. In trying to censure truth we find that truth has no value unless we understand it solely on its own grounds. But how can we praise truth just for its own sake if we do not understand what it means? And the ease with which we are beguiled into censuring what we started out to praise makes it clear that we do *not* know what it means. Yet, these attempts to honor truth have not been idle or without benefit. At the very least we have discovered where not to find the worth of truth, or even its meaning. The final suggestion, that truth should be appreciated solely on its own, is a noble sentiment, but it has no purchase until we can isolate and examine truth in itself.

There are, it seems, many false leads, many misleading paths that turn into cul-de-sacs, in this journey of discovering truth. Before truth can be isolated, the various blind alleyways must first be exposed for what they are.

2

The Myths of Truth

There are common misunderstandings about truth which constitute impediments to any philosophical success in isolating what truth is. Rather in the manner of sweeping away the rubble of the erroneous before building the sound, it is necessary to take stock of the key distortions, not merely to rid the arena of debris, but to elicit in the exposure of these myths a preliminary grasp of what truth in truth is. To identify these as myths, however, is to say more than that they are erroneous. It is also to say that they have, like all myths, a peculiar tenacity on our belief. Myths, as opposed to mere mistakes, have a current of truth in them, and thus they demand evaluation and analysis. Indeed, in a few cases the myths represent the thinking of some of the most influential philosophers in our tradition, and it may seem irreverent to dismiss them so casually. It is not the purpose of this listing to discredit worthy thinkers who have contributed greatly to the illumination of truth by their analyses and arguments, but who, I believe, have fallen prey to subtle but fundamental misunderstandings. The list of these six myths is in no way intended as disrespectful of these powerful thinkers; rather it uses their analyses to point out the pitfalls revealed by the efforts of great minds.

1. *The myth of the autonomy of the object.* The term 'objectivity' has come to designate so fundamental an epistemic virtue that one might think one should be ashamed to be a subject at all. In popular parlance, 'objective' is conceptual virtue, whereas 'subjective' is conceptual vice. The subjective is scarcely different from the prejudiced, the bigoted, the relative. There is in this myth, as in all myths, a sound initial reason for accepting it. Since subjects are variable and are us, and objects are constant and are other, it surely seems advisable to rely on the latter and not the former. We all know countless horror stories of prejudicial

people who have allowed their personal opinions and slants to distort their perceptions, even in cases where the subject is convinced his assessment is unbiased and accurate. Thus, in an admirable attempt to bracket off these damaging elements of subjectivism, the truth is presented as pure objectivity, devoid of all personal distortion. Whatever is contributed by the subject, then, must be vigorously excised or at least sequestered and rendered impotent. The knower strives to achieve, as much as possible, the status of pure receptor. If something must remain of the subject, this is seen as a sad limitation of our finitude. Under the influence of this myth, the empirical becomes triumphant — not, as some would have it, because of a prejudice for the mechanistic, but simply because the empirical seems to favor the object, and because it interprets the subject as a passive recipient.

The myth of the absolute object as a part of knowledge was dispelled by Immanuel Kant, for after his critical analyses it was no longer possible to argue that knowledge could be described solely in terms of the object's influence on a passive subject. But dispelling the myth from epistemology does not ipso facto dispel it from the realm of truth. There seems, in spite of Kant's works and influence, an inescapable bondage to the notion that what is true is objective and what is false is subjective. Under the influence of this misapprehension, one tends to equate truth with fact. No greater disservice to truth or fact is possible.

It is only when this myth is pressed to its logical absurdity that any release from its beguiling fog can be achieved. For if truth is the object, devoid of subject, then truth has no meaning whatever. For then truth would be the same as the object, and would be as unattainable as a subject-free act of knowing. It would never be true that the table is set, the table would just be set; or rather, the truth of the table's being set would be nothing else but the table's being set, which is ridiculous. The truth about the tree cannot be the tree, for the tree itself, as tree, is neither true nor false.

Under the influence of this myth a completely unnatural and sometimes fatal position of thought dominates. Since one's interests and values are obviously not discoverable in external objects, they are branded subjective and hence incapable of being true. Historical traditions can only be prejudicial, and all lofty sentiments are thereby excised on behalf of the true. The truth-seeker, as a consequence, develops a chilly indifference and dispassionate pedanticism, until one wonders why anyone would want to identify with truth at all. Indeed, for some, the predilection for this myth produces a positively perverse conviction that truth simply must be at variance with our interests and our dignity, precisely because such interests and self-esteem are subjective, and the truth, as objective, must therefore oppose them. This produces the vulgar maxim "the baser the truer." Our belief in the nobility, the dignity, and the worth of our species turns out to be subjective illusion and untrue, leaving only the base, the ignoble, and the meaningless as true.

Sadly, even many advocates of the noble are often persuaded by the influence of this myth, and as a consequence have quarantined the term 'truth' from their own wholesome vocabulary. Poets, theologians, preachers, and cultural leaders prefer to speak of dreams and visions, not truth, giving their entire discourse an inauthentic ring. Honest and stalwart defenders of high values, fearing the scorn that is rooted in this myth, embrace it by characterizing their own thoughts as mere beliefs, interpretations, opinions, or revelations. Such language fortifies the dangerous delusion of this myth, for it suggests a formal disjunction between 'truth' as objective and 'belief' as subjective. Under this persuasion, truth is backed deeper and deeper into the dark corner of mere unvalued fact, where no one would ever praise it or honor it. Indeed, in this ignoble corner the independence of truth must eventually disappear.

There is, of course, no defensible reason to maintain this infamous identity of truth with pure objectivity. As Kant did with knowledge surely we can do with truth—that is, we can recognize that objectivity plays a necessary though not a sufficient role in truth. But even as such opportunities present themselves it remains clear that the myth retains considerable power over our minds. Instinctively as we reach for truth we want to foreclose the subjective and enclose the objective. Recognizing such instincts as the product of important though distortive contributions in epistemology passed on to us by the seventeenth and eighteenth centuries may help dispel some of this power, but in the absence of a thorough and successful existential account of truth, the myth of objectivity will probably persist in its delusions.

2. *The myth of the pure subject.* An evil twin to the first myth is the notion that, even if the subject must play a role in truth, such a subject must be lacking in any personal or historical attributes; that the subject is a pure, transcendental function or formal reality, necessary only because human experience requires a subject in order to have an object— not that the subject itself has any content.

The scenario of the second myth usually develops along the following lines. History, tradition, and culture are relative; they obviously differ from subject to subject. Hence, as a resource for truth they are unreliable and should therefore be isolated from any assessment of what is true. This requires the thinker to reflect upon himself inauthentically, that is, as if he had no past or tradition. The myth of the pure subject also suggests that whatever role the subject does play in the discovery of truth, it must be without interest or concern. While not as far-reaching in its nihilism as the first myth, this deluding persuasion tends to make truth precisely that about which we can have no concern or interest. Again, the myth tends to foreclose any interesting sense of truth by making the pure subject just that kind of subject which has no interests.

The prejudice of the second myth, however, is usually most strongly felt in its repudiation of the roles of culture and tradition. Our history, because of its influence—or possibly even indoctrination—becomes an impediment to the achievement of truth just because it is our history. Tradition is thereby seen as a set of blinders which keeps the subject from being the pure subject it ought to be. Of course, the fact that Western civilization is a story of self-critical evaluation is often overlooked. One cannot criticize without a history, for in the absence of historical success there is no reason to be critical in the first place. It is only because I can read, in my history, how respect for critical thinking has achieved such high success in illuminating our world and ourselves that I can learn not only how to be critical but why I ought to be critical. The student who is taught the canons of criticism inherited from such figures as Aristotle, Hume, and Kant can turn these critical powers against the very thinkers who bequeath this precious heritage; but the same student who judges the history of criticism as prejudicial just because it is our history has grossly undervalued the importance of what he has inherited. There are, after all, traditions which do not contain a critical heritage, and archly to equate such traditions with those which provide such canons of thought is simply naive and simplistic.

An example of this myopia can be found in the First Meditation of Descartes, where he tells us that he will try to doubt everything and to forget everything he has learned. But of course, as long as he continues to write in his own language, either Latin or French, he is *not* forgetting what he has learned, for both of these languages are replete with countless presuppositions and classical influences. Not merely the words he uses, but the grammar, syntax, and style determine to some extent how he will think. Surely his notion of substance is influenced, if not determined, by the syntactical rules governing a language which uses nouns and verbs. Thus, no matter how hard he tries, the "I" which Descartes isolates is not a pure subject which functions solely as knower, but a richly endowed subject influenced and characterized by the very language he uses to express his own dubiety. There is nothing unfortunate about this, although Descartes himself might have thought so. Indeed without a culturally rich language no criticism or methodic doubting is possible. What is wrong is merely the arrogant assumption that one can inquire *ab novo,* and such arrogance contributes greatly to this myth.

The greatest danger in this second myth, however, remains the presumption that the passivity of formal mind approaches truth more surely than a mind enriched by history and culture. This dreadful error is unfortunately not restricted to philosophy. The feminists who seem sincerely to believe they can imagine the purely natural and untainted woman are committing the same error, for whatever a woman is or whatever a male might be, they cannot be anything at all without a culture. The political theorists who imagine they can isolate what a pure, untainted, cultureless man might be are also deeply mistaken. The entire methodology of seeking to isolate *any* notion from its historical meaning is not only bad thinking, it is also morally dangerous. The objection that such cultural dependence is chauvinistic is ill conceived, for accepting a tradition never means surrendering one's critical functions. What threatens is rather the devaluing of truth, and with such devaluing comes the inevitable stagnation of nihilistic indifference. Under the influence of this myth, not only is truth without value, but what is worse, value is without truth.

3. *The myth of the extraworldly.* It is sadly amusing to hear so many contemporaries protest that the medieval world suffers from an overemphasis on the 'otherworldly'. In point of fact no one is as otherworldly as the contemporary analytic epistemologist who couches all argumentation in the language of 'possible worlds'. The suggestion is that one can somehow get out of this world and stand, somewhere, and look around the vast display of possible worlds, among which is the lowly actual world. But where is one standing when one conceives or projects such worlds? Is not the very imagination or creative mind that projects such possibilities in this world? Strictly speaking, there can be only one world, *this* world, and to speak or think as if this world were

merely one among many is inconceivable. I cannot imagine another world in which my thirst exists but I do not. How then can I *think* of another world which, perforce, must contain my own thinking, since it is my thought that produces it? It may well be that the term 'world' when used strictly and precisely simply permits of no plurality. There cannot be a plurality of possible worlds, since only this world contains the minds which are the origins of such speculation.

Nevertheless, the contemporary argot is to speak in terms of possible worlds, and this way of speaking—and hence thinking—provides a deadly and distortive perception which I identify as the myth of the extraworldly. This is a dangerous myth precisely because in reaching beyond the world it reaches beyond sense. Under the influence of this myth a nonexistent, indeed impossible, place is conceived as that which is most important. The ability to conjure possible worlds becomes the podium from which the concertmaster directs all the instruments of thinking, so that in the absence of this figure only cacophony and disharmony is possible. But this podium and this concertmaster do not exist, for they are treated as belonging to no world whatsoever, as beyond all worlds. It is from this inconceivable podium beyond all worlds that alternative structures are entertained and assessed as worlds. The focus of truth is hence beyond the world, but since truth can be grounded only in the world, there is no truth about truth. So what would make things true is itself not true.

The distortion to thought that this 'otherworldly' myth fosters is devastating. There is surely nothing wrong in speculation about possibilities; indeed such speculation is essential for understanding logic itself. But it is not at all obvious that speculation about contrary-to-fact conditionals entails a plurality of possible worlds. The term 'world' is sadly used in two senses here, the first sense meaning 'realm' and the second meaning that which grounds the real. The myth is thus exposed as an instance of the fallacy of ambiguity.

The temptation of philosophers to seek out some neutral zone, untouched by history, influence, culture, or tradition, is a powerful but fatal lure endemic to the nature of speculation. Such a zone cannot exist, but it is imagined as existing by those who abstract themselves by techniques of mental self-deception, arriving at a critical stage of reflection where all things are strange.

The fault may in part lie with G. W. Leibniz, who introduced the vocabulary of possible worlds to achieve his theodicy. But if the error was seeded in Leibniz it surely has been thwarted by thinkers like Kant and Heidegger. Kant's method is so remarkable in this regard that it deserves mention here. He never finds it necessary to step out of the world of ordinary experience and wonder; rather he insists that philosophy must always be done transcendentally or critically—that is, we accept the world as it is and then ask what must be presupposed in order to account for it. By raising the question in this way, we never lose sight of the world we live in; rather our everyday experience itself becomes the focus of inquiry, and the question is merely that of how such experience is possible. Heidegger later develops the remarkable doctrine that human existence is always already (a priori) in-the-world (*In-der-welt-sein*). Thus, for Heidegger, the world is never conceived as some external reality outside the knowing subject, but rather contains the subject as an essential way in which we exist within the world. Thus we do not know the world, we rather know within the world.

These brief observations from the history of philosophy are not meant as resolutions or answers; they are made merely to provoke a sense of the lofty status which this question has. It may be that Kant and Heidegger have shown the weakness of Leibniz's logic of possible worlds, but if so, the argument is even more significant when applied to the contemporary analytic thinker who projects possible worlds as if his own mind need not be in a world to achieve truth.

The myth unfortunately is not restricted to professional philosophers who may or may not be making an error in modal logic. The myth supports the common, everyday attitude expressed by such disarming questions as "Who's to say . . . ?" or "By what right do we make judgments . . . ?" These questions are often raised among the pampered and self-indulgent who rely on the dazzling oddness of their questions to create a miasma of unalloyed brilliance. What is distressing is not that the uninformed may think such pompous questions undermine all authority, but that the concerned and diligent thinker may find himself disarmed before these curious flank assaults on his reasoning. Who are we to say? Why, we are beings in the world, whose thought and experience within the world provide whatever authority comes from good reasoning and proper experience. The difficulty is not that there is no answer to these oracular questions, but that the answer is too obvious to be used. The misological suggestion that all judgments are intrasystematic and hence have no authority unless one accepts the system, rather than that judgments are within the world, is a myth, and like all myths has great power to dissuade thinkers who may be unalert to the deviousness involved.

When Nietzsche entreats us in the Prologue to *Thus Spoke Zarathustra* to return to and love the earth, he may have been speaking against overly celestial metaphysicians, but his protest is actually more applicable to the contemporary persuasion that to think is to achieve some weird and fantastic podium beyond the world. As with Archimedes' search for a fulcrum with which he could move the world, the point is usually lost entirely; for Archimedes was seeking to illustrate the power of the lever, not to find the fulcrum. He knew quite well there was no magical or mysterious fulcrum; rather, he was attempting to show us how to think about levers. Possibilities are essential to our thinking, but they do not bring with them an infinity of possible worlds, nor in thinking of them do we somehow lose our own place in the only world that counts, this one.

4. *The myth of the sentence.* If you ask a contemporary analytic philosopher to examine the meaning of truth he will inevitable begin by analyzing a sentence which he knows or assumes to be true. This seems an entirely rational and coherent thing to do. After all, if I want to know about chocolate it might make sense to begin with a chocolate cake and remove those elements which make it a mere cake, to find the residue to be chocolate. Why not, then, if one's goal is truth, begin with a sentence that is true and remove all other elements such as syntax, grammar, and even words, so that the remains will show us truth by itself? There is, indeed, an advantage to this procedure, for by introducing the sentence, it avoids the danger of leaving truth in the mists of sheer objectivity or the darkness of pure subjectivity. Truth is neither subject nor object, nor is it "in" either. Rather, it is the link or connection between the two, and hence has a status independent of them.

Sentences depend upon specific languages, so that the German "Der Hund ist klein" and the English "The dog is small" provide two different sentences, but the underlying or imbedded proposition is the same. Bertrand Russell thus defines the proposition as that which is true or false; and it is the presence of the proposition in both the English and the German sentences which make them true or false in a derived sense. But even propositions cannot *be* the truth; for if propositions or sentences are either true or false then what makes them true rather than false must be something other than the proposition itself. What makes the proposition true is the correspondence to what is the case. Only propositions, strictly speaking, can correspond or not correspond, and hence only propositions can be true or false. It may seem odd to insist that what makes a proposition true is itself not true, but the reasoning here is sound. What is the case — or even 'the object' — itself is neither true nor false, since in order to have truth one needs both a claim and what the claim is about. Thus propositions, and indirectly sentences, alone can be true.

The soundness of this argumentation is not in question, but its relevance to understanding the meaning of truth surely is. One difficulty with this analysis is the assumption that the proposition or sentence is finished or static when analyzed. The analysis begins with an already extant proposition, as if it were an existing entity, which then either corresponds to what is said or does not. Sentences, it seems, are actual entities and propositions are abstract entities. Truth is therefore itself not an entity but a relation between two entities, rather like 'being to the left of' is a relation, and as such has no metaphysical status except in light of the two entities related. Truth is therefore a relation between two entities, the proposition and 'what is the case'. But the analysis depends on the proposition being conceived as an entity independent of its speaker. It is almost as if we must somehow imagine the sentence in which the proposition is imbedded as written down and having a life of its own there on the page. Of course what is written on the page is not a sentence but a mere collection or series of marks which is interpreted as a sentence. The meaning of a sentence requires an interpretive mind to make it possible as a candidate for correctly representing or corresponding to what is the case.

This requires us to think of language solely as communication. When either written or spoken, language communicates an interpretation of sounds or symbols on a page as meaningful because it communicates either to another mind or itself the correspondence between the sentence and what is the case. It is highly unlikely, however, that language can be seen primarily as communication, and certainly language cannot be seen as merely communication. Further, how a proposition, which is an abstract entity, can indeed correspond to what exists in the world is difficult if not impossible to imagine. If what is communicated is a meaning rather than a correspondence, then the focus of truth shifts from the correspondence to the meaning. The correspondence theory of truth depends upon the communicative theory of language, which is highly dubious. For what is communicated? Sentences? Meanings?

Propositions? But according to this theory, all three presuppose language, and language cannot communicate what it presupposes; or rather, language cannot *be* mere communication of what it presupposes, for how can it communicate what does not yet exist?

Furthermore, this notion of truth is extremely narrow: it refers only to the special and limited sense of truth which can be analyzed in terms of simple direct assertions and their correspondence to simple facts. Truth must be more broadly conceived than this, as will be argued in subsequent chapters. However, its narrowness reveals the weakness of this notion of truth. The sentential approach still seems to treat the abstract entity, a proposition, as somehow containing truth *already*. This is troubling because it seems circular. If one begins with the analysis of a proposition by itself there is no guarantee the proposition is true (unless it is an analytic proposition). So we must begin with a true proposition and say that the truth of the proposition lies in its correspondence to what is the case. But of course that is to abandon the proposition or sentence. If truth must be understood in terms other than the sentence or the proposition — and it must if false sentences are possible — then it is dubious to maintain that truth in any way lies in the nature of the proposition or that the meaning of truth can be revealed by the dissection of a sentence.

The argument is, I take it, that it is not the proposition itself which yields truth but the correspondence of the proposition to what is the case. But this sounds suspiciously redundant. It is not the proposition which yields truth but the truth in the proposition which yields truth. This surely cannot be doubted, but it seems to make the term 'in the proposition' unnecessary. For if only those propositions that correspond are true, one says nothing else but that true propositions are true. In other words, the analysis becomes nothing more than mere word-substitution.

There is also the lingering suspicion that one has here confused the criterion with the meaning. It may be clear that what makes a sentence true is its correspondence, but that does not tell us what truth is, it merely tells us when truth is. To say, however, that truth means something other than the sentence itself obviously is to go beyond the sentence.

To speak of the myth of the sentence is not to speak of the myth of language. Truth cannot be found in the dissection of a sentence, but truth remains linked to language. Truth cannot be independent of language, nor is language meaningful without truth. We cannot equate language with mere sentences, and surely not with mere propositions. Why this is so exceeds the range of the present chapter.

5. *The myth of the system.* Few experiences are more irritating than to see theorists speculating on their "system of philosophy." The sheer arrogance of those who invent edifices of "truth" is excelled only by their incapacity to learn what is important from the world. There may be systems of explanation, but there is no system of truth, nor is truth "in" a system. To be sure, any adequate account of the world and our existence must include an account of truth itself, but to identify truth with the system, which is the common error, is woefully bad thinking. Truth is not a system.

The fault, in part, may lie with lazy and improper reading and teaching of the history of philosophy, in which dreary and repetitive reference to "Aristotle's system" or "Kant's system" cannot help but establish in a student's mind the envy of such fame. A system is, after all, an attempt to explain the entire truth, and who could be more admired than someone capable of doing that? But there is little to admire in what can be done by everyone equally well. There are few things easier than to invent, devise, create, or speculatively imagine a "system," and to package it with a cunning vocabulary and attractive terminology and launch it like a hot-air balloon above the heads of easily impressed onlookers.

There may indeed be, as Kant suggests, a natural architectonic to human reason, but it is still improper to speak of Kant's "system." Football coaches may have systems of defense, nations may have systems of government, businesses may have systems of accounting or book-keeping; but thinkers, strictly speaking, cannot have systems of truth because it is always possible to ask: "But is the system true?" It is sometimes protested that the truth of a system is internal to the system, but this is a misunderstanding. Systems, to the extent they are legitimate, are constructed to arrive at or illuminate the truth; their construction does not produce the truth. Systems are not methodologies, either; for good thinkers develop identifiable methodologies to get at the truth, which again means that the methodology is other than the truth. But the illegitimate use of the system views systems not as a means to *get at* the truth but as *enclosing* the truth. This is a dangerous myth in part because it attracts by reducing truth to what can be managed. And this of course is also the reason why the identification of truth with systems sustains such pompous and unwarranted arrogance. Hegel, of course, seems to understand his "system" in precisely this way; and although he is a great thinker, he must be brought to task. There may indeed be a vast, internally supportive system of *knowledge,* which is what Hegel brilliantly defends in his argument. But whether the same intersystematic authority can be found in *truth* is quite another matter.

For truth, in order for it to be truth, demands its autonomy. The world has more to tell us than we have to tell the world. There is something remarkably captivating about a system. It binds precisely as it develops. A system provides magnificent illusions of freedom and accountability; in explaining everything it uncovers nothing. Yet, the myth of the systematic may have the greatest allure of all the myths precisely because the truth-seeker cannot avoid the inevitability of order and logic. Reason is effective only because of systemic order, and without reason there is no truth. Yet, the very notion that a thinker creates a system or builds one is counter to the idea of truth as autonomous.

Out of what materials do thinkers construct their systems? Surely they build on what they have learned. But if what they learn precedes the system, which it must, the truth cannot come from the system. Yet, one cannot have truth without organized thought which itself may have been not learned but simply directly intuited or reasoned. If by 'system' one means a structured or organized approach to learning, this is surely acceptable, perhaps even inevitable. For in the absence of such organization there is no thematic unity, and the observations and insights of the thinker will be random or even wanton. And so the legitimate need for some systemization cannot be denied. But the term 'system' has come to mean far more than this; it has come to mean a project or a construct which is equated with truth itself, and that is a dangerous myth.

An outgrowth of this myth is the jungle fecundity of multifarious "isms" which so plague the fields of academic thought that the weeds have choked out the flowers. Unfortunately this proliferation of isms has become acceptable practice, and the consequent identification of thought with misological labeling has turned the noble task of thinking into an ignoble chore of sticking on tags. It seems now that the supreme faculty of the professors is nothing more than nailing up plaques over dead systems lying about in ubiquitous heaps. Do you seek to understand Kant? Find his label—transcendental idealist—look it up in a dictionary, and you will know all there is to know. From monism to existentialism, from Marxism to dualism, the student wanders about among these labels as among tombstones in a graveyard. Philosophy has become a series of epitaphs marking the dead. For death is the only quality noticeable in the once lively thought now catalogued in the ever-thickening encyclopedia of philosophical systems identified with the suffix -ism. Indeed, even this very protest cannot escape this grim graffiti, for it shall be forever tagged: anti-ismism.

One deadly threat inherent in this pedagogic silliness is the loss of thought. We consider only what a thinker says, not why he says it; and even less do we attend to the agony and the life that prompts the thinker to probe into his own questioning and wonder. With the coming of this myth the sun, truth, is eclipsed by the moon of systemic ismism, and the result is noonday darkness. Consider the silliness of this procedure. In seeking to understand Descartes we find the label 'dualism' hovering about his works like a bad smell. In some convenient handbook or on some available software in our computers we can find the definition of dualism as a doctrine maintaining the existence of two separate and distinct entities, mind and body. We also find an asterisk—or the green light flashes on the screen—which refers us to the warning that dualism has been replaced by the identity theory. The investigator into isms is thus not unlike the supermarket shopper who must decide between plums and grapes for the family snack. At no time is the shopper of these fruited isms ever made aware of the burden of Descartes' reasoning. And if one begins with this approach, no attempt to go back to the texts and resuscitate the arguments can succeed, because the embalming fluid has done its work. Descartes is not a dualist. Rather he is a thinker who reflects that reasoning is obviously different from feeling, and who then is obligated to account for this difference. He appeals to the notion of separate entities. It is necessary, of course, for us to challenge this thinking, and excellent critics have done so. But good critics of Descartes do not attack his conclusions but his reasoning, and in order to criticize his reasoning one must affirm the logical persuasion that led Descartes to the original distinction. This is to think along with the thinker. To approach his thought from the mere advertising on the package is to avoid philosophy altogether. Ism kills thought.

Truth cannot consist of answers only, divorced from questioning. To separate the result from the asking is to reduce thought to claims, and the prejudice follows that one claim is just as good as another. That thinkers may just possibly care about truth is rendered irrelevant. How can one claim among so many lay claim to truth if all claims are possible answers? Indeed the prior question, "answers to what?" is rarely even asked. The result is the *reductio ad absurdum* committed by an under-graduate who once wrote: "Descartes believes in two substances because he is a dualist." The ism has now been raised from the common level of a mere tag to the royal level of a reason. Of such myths are many *F*s conceived and born.

Though it may not seem apparent, all systems are essentially mecha-nistic. A system thinks the world in terms of the metaphor of a machine. Indeed, thinking itself under this misappraisal is merely the schemata of an elaborate electronic device. Machines operate successfully because of their systematic order; and an explanative system operates like a machine. The parts function in terms of their service to the mechanism as such, and the machine, in turn, is an elaborate tool to serve some-thing else. By itself, no machine has any meaning. Yet all systems use the world including themselves, as a machine.

A few may object that there are animistic systems or even systems of evolution which cannot be reduced to a mechanistic metaphor. But even these elaborate systems are questionable just because they explain in exactly the same way that one explains a machine. If you pull this lever, this cog will turn, causing this pulley to operate. Animistic or evolutionary systems merely hide these parts with a fig leaf of distracting language. To speak of life forces in exactly the same way one talks about the forces of gravity or the magnetic fields that activate iron filings is to reduce life to a machine, regardless of how sanctimonious the terminology. The warm, living, vibrant, loving, lustful, and sensuous sinner known as a human being can be explained, it seems, by an elaborate system of electronic impulses, microchips in the brain, transistors, data banks, and sparks that energize. It used to be one would feel offended if called an animal; now such vitality is precious, for the greater reduction is that we do not even have the spark of life; what sparks is electricity, and rather than having the passions of an animal we now have the impulse of an electronic mechanism.

The rapid growth of the sophistication of computers fuels the inferno of this raging myth. Mechanism, even if electronic, can contain no truth whatsoever; for truth then becomes merely an assigned variable. These machines are wonderful to those who can use them successfully without becoming overawed by the prodigality of their performance. But instead we have systems of "artificial intelligence" and "thinking machines" which easily seduce the unalert into believing that machines really do think, so that in thinking we are really machines. In part this silliness is the result of depicting thought and truth as systemic; for a computer is, after all, a system. But there is no truth in a computer.

This myth may lead to such gross errors as seeking to depict thought as mechanistic, but it has a further symptom in the development of political ideologies. All ideologies are systemic, and as such they are all mechanistic. The horror one feels in the written presence of a Robespierre, a Lenin, or a Himmler is due not to their wickedness but to their brilliant indifference. Machines care not whom they mangle; there is no cruelty or lust in a machine. But the dreaded reigns of the incorruptibles terrorize all the more because of the passionate dispassion that motivates their tyranny. Hitler himself may have hated Jews and Poles and Russians, but his henchmen, who made the system work, shared the mechanical view of an inevitable system necessarily unfolding. Robespierre, Lenin, Stalin, Himmler, and others were quite willing to put millions to their deaths simply because it was systemically proper to do so. The Nazis are often depicted as deep haters, and some of them doubtless were, but what made that movement so foul was the lack of hatred, for hatred is at least a human emotion. These men and women were nihilists; they thought of themselves merely as parts of a system, and hence crimes did not matter.

For them, the state too is a machine; it is a justice machine. It is conceived by all ideologues—that is, system-makers—as a mechanism for bringing about justice. In revolutionary machines, since the tradition is overthrown, justice itself is merely a part of the machine: power. What makes these regimes so dreadful is not that justice is arbitrary, but that justice like everything else is merely a systemic part, and inevitable.

But, you say, it is silly to fear a machine. It is not silly to fear a feral beast whose blood-lust or fear or hunger may motivate savagery; machines, however, as instruments have no personal interests, and hence cannot be feared. The analysis here seems to have gone astray, for certainly the likes of Lenin and Robespierre who could calmly sign death warrants for millions out of a mechanistic sense of inevitability should be feared. If they are interpreted as mechanists, and if machines are not to be feared, then why should they be feared?

The fear is not of the machine itself but of becoming a machine. The wicked among us can be feared, despised, punished, and forgiven. But the threat that develops beyond us is evil. Evil means that which is impelled by nonhuman motives. It is true that machines cannot terrorize, but it is a form of terror to think like a machine. If we are thinking of the human mind, then a machine is truly horrifying. To allow one's sensitivity to truth to become articulated as a machine or as a system is more than a myth, it is a danger.

Recently a convicted murderer on death row in the state of Florida complained in a television interview that his crimes were the result of a fault in the psyche, which, he added, should have been spotted by the experts and then fixed, so he would not have to endure the punishment. After all, you fix a faulty transmission, so why not fix a faulty psyche? And indeed the death-row inmate is quite correct in his reasoning. For the growth of systems, both in metaphysics and in governments, has resulted in such deep philosophical perversion that it has become common to think of the mind and the soul as a machine. Machines should not be punished, they should be fixed.

The allure of an ideology or a system is very strong, particularly in the political realm. For it is curiously comforting to blame faulty systems for all our woes and argue that one system can replace another, and we need only choose the right—or even merely a new—system to achieve happiness for all. But even if systems could produce justice or happiness, they certainly cannot produce truth, for truth is not something produced but something revealed or discovered. Yet the lure of the system, as a myth, persists in spite of all such insights, partly because those who think about systems refuse to accept that any other kind of thinking is possible. A Marxist, for example, insists that his system is merely an inevitable replacement of capitalism, which is itself a system. Perhaps capitalism is a system, but only in the sense of an established series of interconnections, not in the sense of a speculatively projected description. Private property may not be inevitable and surely there are abuses to it, but it was never conceived as a speculative alternative or an ideology, which was then adopted because of its systemic superiority. There is no truth at all in any purely speculative system or ideology; but there is always some truth, even when shackled in dreadful institutionalization, in any tradition. The evil of ideological terror rests on its systemic untruth; the redemptive power of a revitalized and renewed tradition is based on truth.

In spite of these warnings, it must be admitted that there is a legitimate use of the designation 'system' and even of the hateful suffix 'ism'; but the legitimate uses and the illegitimate uses are distinguished by so subtle a difference that these terms should be avoided whenever possible.

6. *The myth of knowledge.* The final and most pestiferous of these

myths of truth is that truth is knowledge. There is no doubt that knowledge is of supreme importance to the philosopher as well as all men who seek to live thoughtfully in the world. Many philosophers actually refer to their task as the quest for knowledge rather than truth, and only a fool would prefer ignorance to what can be known. Nor can one deny that truth and knowledge are closely intertwined. But though close they are still different, and it is important to note that the praise of the great figures is reserved for truth, not knowledge. Knowledge surely deserves its own accolades. Perhaps, even, in a utilitarian sense, knowledge is more beneficial than truth. But in the sense of what is of autonomous worth, it is truth, and not knowledge, which must rank supreme.

A few random remarks may initiate the understanding of this difference. The opposite of knowledge is ignorance; the opposite of the true is the untrue or the false. Ignorance may be excused, but the untrue, never. Knowledge characterizes those who have it, that is, subjects. But truth is neither subject nor object. Knowledge presupposes truth in the sense that one cannot be said to know what is false. In other words, to know is to know what is true.

And because what I know is true it seems the surest route to the meaning of truth is to be found in an analysis of knowing. But this approach, though greatly favored by most contemporary epistemologists, is not only misleading, it is also dangerous because it is backwards. Knowledge does not give us truth, rather truth is what makes knowledge possible. To approach truth by way of knowledge is to confuse the victory with the reward, the hero with his medals. One cannot reach the proper understanding of truth by the analysis of knowledge precisely because the former is presupposed by the latter. In formal analysis, whatever is ultimately presupposed by anything always outranks it, for that which is presupposed is what makes the other possible in the first place.

If I say, "I know that it is true that men suffer," it may seem, as was noted above, that I am saying nothing else than I know men suffer, and perhaps I am only saying men suffer. If this is correct, the expression 'it is true that' adds nothing, and is hence meaningless. But this is because the expression merely makes explicit what is already assumed, and hence rather than being meaningless is the very foundation of all meaning. To say truth is presupposed in knowledge is to deny that truth can be approached solely through the analysis of knowledge. That it is presupposed means that it is more deeply hidden and that it is so fundamental that the simple analysis of knowing, a difficult task in itself, cannot yield its meaning.

Knowledge can be used; truth is never used. Oddly, however, the inverse of these statements is revealing: ignorance is not useful, though my own ignorance can be used against me by others; but the untrue or the false is very useful. For the false, as deceit, beguiles, and in the hands of the unscrupulous is a potent instrument of political and psychological mastery. The very fact that the untrue can be abused by the cunning raises the temptation to seek out the meaning of truth *via negativa* and to try to get at truth by analyzing the false. (The true is that which is not false.) Though one can learn a great deal through such methods of negation, the truth of truth must be approached positively, for, as was noted above, the false has a thousand faces, the true but one.

The recognition of this myth suggests that the proper approach to truth is not through knowledge but through ignorance, or rather, through a certain kind of ignorance, called "Socratic ignorance." This special philosophical ignorance is the foundation of inquiry, and it is important because it first provokes our understanding of the essential meaning of truth as a beckoning. Truth beckons. And this is the most telling revelation of the mythical status of knowledge as truth. The great glory of knowledge is precisely that it does not beckon. It is because knowledge must be of the true that the truth is incarcerated by knowledge. Knowledge freezes truth into a lifeless necessity. Truth is of interest not to the *knower* but rather to the *seeker*. The knower, in knowing, by necessity must overlook the truth because knowledge, in enclosing the light, has smothered the flame.

Knowledge can be imparted to another, but truth cannot be passed from one to another like bits of information. When one claims to impart the truth what one really means is that one imparts knowledge, which must be true by definition. But truth itself is not imparted or even communicated. Throughout this inquiry it is important to sustain the distinction: what is *true* is not itself always *truth*. One may die for truth, but rarely is any single true fact worthy of a death. Yet, this distinction is so often overlooked that to do so is to be captive to the deception of a myth.

These myths of truth are not mere errors. Like all myths they have a persistent appeal; and like all myths they are not entirely without some truth in them. This provisional codification of them may help, however, to direct attention to the peculiar nature of truth itself by isolating it from the distraction of the usurpers. As the myths are uncovered the elusive but radiant essence of truth beckons like a light in the dark fog of deception. Truth, for all its obvious wealth and allure, is notoriously difficult to grasp, for it is surrounded by deep prejudices, which are the six myths, and is girded by a seemingly impenetrable paradox. The myths tend to wither away when exposed, but the paradox is a part of the essence of truth itself and hence must be confronted directly.

3

The Paradox of Truth

It would seem that if any notion were accessible to the inquirer it should be truth itself. Since truth is presupposed by all knowledge, surely it must itself be of inescapable clarity and ready comprehension. When one says "this is true" there can be no doubt what is meant, and if almost everyone obviously *does* know what it means to say "this is true" it seems an outrageous assault on common sense to assert there is anything mysterious or unclear about what truth means. It may be hard to define, but then so are all simple notions like 'up', 'no', 'like', and 'it'—but the difficulty in definition is merely a matter of closeness. The problem is, there are no other terms more immediate and obvious than 'no', and so to define it one must, perforce, use terms less obvious, and that renders the description somewhat lacking. So, too, with 'truth'. Since we all know what it means—after all, we all use it correctly often enough—why should there be any problem?

This common-sense criticism is, in part, quite valid. This inquiry is not an investigation into a new notion which needs explanation in order to be utilized correctly. Nor is truth a terribly complex notion like 'society' which presents difficulty because of its diverse modes. We do indeed know how to use the term 'true', and this must mean we understand its proper usage and to some extent its meaning. But our knowing how to use the word 'true' correctly in a sentence does not mean we understand the full depth and range of meaning in the term 'truth'.

Indeed, the task of raising the very question of truth is itself beset with a troubling paradox which threatens to leave the philosopher in the same position as the untroubled common speaker in the above paragraph, abandoning the problem altogether as undeserving of the search. This paradox may be stated as a variant of the paradox of analysis: the search for truth must either begin with something — usually a sentence — which is true; or it must begin from ignorance. Ignorance will never yield truth; but to begin with a true sentence is to begin where one should end. Either truth simply becomes knowledge, or it is so deeply imbedded in a true sentence that it can never mean anything except what we already know — that the sentence is true. The problem is, how we come to know the truth of the sentence has to do not with truth itself but with what the sentence is about. If, for example, I assert that men suffer, the evidence I have for this claim is about my experience of the human species: it is about human beings and suffering — it has nothing to do with truth. Indeed, if I assert such a claim in ordinary conversation the focus of attention is solely upon the wretchedness or sacrificial nobility of the human condition, and not at all on what truth means.

Suppose, however, one says "This sentence contains five words." I not only listen to this claim to learn what is said, I also *consider* the sentence as made up of words and count them. Perhaps truth is like this: there are many sentences which contain five words, but we do not notice this fact until our attention is somehow directed toward the number of words. So although the sentence "William Shakespeare wrote *King Lear*" also has five words, only an extraordinary device draws our attention to this uninteresting fact. The sentence rather is about the authorship of a great play. But if asked we can count the words; so if asked we can reflect on what is meant by "this is true" and find there is no mystery, only a difference of interest. Normally we do not worry about the number of words in a sentence, unless there are simply too many, and because of this disinterest we may not readily note the number of words in any given sentence. But we can always count them. Normally, too, we simply do not make specific what we mean by 'truth' when we say "this is true," but, like the word-counting, it is available to us if we focus our attention on it.

Of course, the difficulty is that focusing our attention on truth is far more demanding than focusing on the number of words in a sentence. Again, the point contains much that is valid: we *can* direct our attention to a true sentence either in terms of what makes it true or solely in terms of what the sentence informs us about. Is, then, the sentence really two sentences, the one about Shakespeare writing *Lear* and the other about the *truth* of Shakespeare writing *Lear*? It would seem rather that there is only one sentence which can be attended to in two ways: as a source of information about who wrote *Lear* and as a source of understanding truth.

But here the paradox deepens. What makes the sentence true is that Shakespeare wrote *Lear*. But that is also what provides us information concerning the authorship of the play. What the sentence is about, however, cannot be the truth of the sentence. For we observe carefully: if the *truth* of the sentence "Shakespeare wrote *King Lear*" is that Shakespeare wrote *King Lear*, what is *true* is not the sentence but the fact. In losing the quotation marks we have gone from a sentence to a fact. But the truth cannot be the fact, since the fact can occur without any awareness or understanding of it. The fact cannot be false, hence how can it be true? Somehow, by losing the quotation marks we have lost the truth.

This may seem playful rather than serious. But the paradox remains: truth seems to require that I know it in order to understand it, but I can only know it if it is already true. The very requirement that a sentence *be* true if we are to analyze it *as* true renders the analysis circular.

Perhaps then the option from ignorance should be reconsidered. What is truth to the inquirer? Is it knowledge? It would seem obvious that knowledge is what the seeker after truth desires, so why does he not say so? Why not identify the inquirer as the knowledge-seeker rather than the truth-seeker? But is this identification accurate? Perhaps in seeking truth the inquirer is *not* seeking knowledge. But this seems absurd, for surely if I am seeking the *truth* about the author of *King Lear* I necessarily am seeking to *know* who the author of *King Lear* is. Perhaps. But this analysis of the ignorant inquirer has opened up a rich suggestion. Perhaps the *true* is essential for knowledge but the *truth* is essential for inquiry.

There is a famous story told by Lessing in which he imagines that God visits him in observable guise and offers him a reward for his goodness. In his right hand, God holds truth, and in his left he holds the search for truth. God asks Lessing which of the two he desires. Lessing claims his answer would be: "I'll take what is in the left hand, and leave the truth for God alone." This is not a mere charming story about Lessing's humility or his acceptance of finitude. The story is deeply paradoxical. For if Lessing genuinely desires to seek the truth, then is he not disingenuous in turning down the offer of truth itself? If I desire gold and someone offers me gold or a stake in a possible gold claim, I would take the gold. By denying God's offer of truth Lessing seems to be denying any *meaningful* sense of a search for truth. Why search for truth if, when offered it, one turns it down?

Yet this fable of Lessing's suggests a deeper insight than mere frustration with someone who does not know what he wants. There is the suggestion in this little story that only an infinite being can possess truth, and that to accept the right-handed offer is to forfeit one's humanity. There is also the stronger suggestion that truth is of value to us only as an ideal; that the actual possession of truth (knowledge?) renders it *less* valuable. But these suggestions merely deepen the paradox, they do not resolve it. It seems as if the formula is this: "wanting x" is somehow superior to "having x." One wonders if the regress continues. Is it even better "to want to want to want x"? But this is absurd.

It may be absurd to continue the regress, but the original suggestion is still important. It is possible to maintain that wanting x is better than having x. Many players enjoy the struggle to achieve victory more than winning. Some men woo in joy and possess in sorrow. Why should not the search for truth outrank the possession of it? If we know the butler did it, how can we enjoy the mystery story? But if *this* is all that is meant, the praise of truth has again been misplaced. Rather we should praise the *search* for truth. Truth itself is like the marriage contract, it takes the fun out of the fun. Furthermore it seems to equate truth with a mirage which, though it excites the thirsty traveler and beckons him to the spot, once there the illusion vanishes and the thirst remains as trenchant as before. One certainly does not think highly of a mirage, which promises only false hopes. And if it is argued that the search for truth in any way outranks truth itself, we must question whether we are not dealing with mere self-indulgence. Children can fantasize and amuse themselves by pretense, but if the search for truth is the search for that which becomes unimportant in the possession, then the truth-seeker is no different from the illusion-seeker. Indeed, why should the truth-seeker be of more importance than any other seeker, such as the pleasure-seeker or the fame-seeker? To argue that the seeking itself is what gives truth its worth is merely to point out a curious psychological fact about some people, that they enjoy the chase more than the kill, and *what* they choose matters not one whit. This makes truth little more than a rabbit.

Of course, it is quite possible that Lessing simply misleads us in this story. Perhaps his fantasy would have been more beneficial to our understanding were he to have accepted truth itself. The two horns of the dilemma seem to be these: (1) if I *have* truth, I *know,* and this inquiry should be into knowledge rather than truth, and (2) if I *long* for truth but do not accept it when it comes, this essay should probe into the psychologically interesting concept of longing, not truth. One can see the value in knowledge, and one can appreciate the value in seeking, but truth itself is neither. Why not simply forget truth and focus on searching and knowing?

In the *Symposium*, Socrates compares this dilemma of truth with the similar dilemma in loving the beautiful. The lover longs for his beloved, hence must lack; yet he also possesses the beloved, hence cannot long for it. Socrates suggests that the lover must be understood as both possessing and lacking beauty at the same time even though this seems to throw the law of contradiction out of the discussion. He then draws a parallel between the lover of beauty and the lover of truth, claiming that both must possess and lack. This echoes Juliet's famous remark, "and yet I long but for the thing I have", which suggests that even fourteen-year-old girls realize something is wrong. But what is wrong with Juliet is that she is in love. What is wrong with Socrates is he loves the truth.

The Socratic version of the paradox is too often overlooked, because of the more spectacular teachings of the dialogue. Socrates obviously means for us to wonder about the paradox, not to solve it. But are not paradoxes precisely those puzzles which are presented so that they may be solved? Or is it that there is a new paradox altogether, that truth is revealed in paradox, not in answers or solutions?

The Socratic version raises the fascinating question: is searching inconsistent with having? Is having always the end of longing? Juliet continues to long for Romeo even after she has won him entirely. But that is a love story. Indeed, it is even worse than that, it is a dramatized, fictional love story written in poetry. But the *Symposium* is a piece of philosophical literature, and they seem to say the same thing. It is not easy to understand exactly what is meant by the Socratic equation of love for beauty with the love for truth, but there is no doubt the dialogue takes the comparison seriously. It would certainly seem that longing precludes possession, and that to have something is not to want it. But this merely intensifies the problem. The appeal to Socrates has not eased the question at all. As usual, when Socrates is brought in, what seemed clear becomes muddy, and this reflection on the paradox of truth is no exception. Rather, by reminding ourselves of the Socratic version of the paradox we avoid the suspicion that perhaps the paradox is merely a confusion based upon how language communicates reality. Socrates, in comparing truth to beauty in terms of how we love both, has given the paradox considerable prestige. But there is also much insight in the Socratic version. Socrates seems to suggest, by the analogy with the love of beauty, that there is not only a paradox in truth but truth in paradox. That is, if the Socratic insight is correct, truth is achieved not merely by thinking in terms of true answers, but by seeking to understand the unresolvable questions, that is, the paradox. Just as love cannot be resolved by satisfying an urge, so truth cannot be achieved by satisfying an interrogation. Answers are not truth; rather questioning is truth. Answers may be true, but they are not the truth.

The realization that *truth* is found in questioning and the *true* is found in answers helps solve the dilemma posed by the characterization of Socrates' execution as a death for truth.

Men and women of a thousand different creeds have suffered and died for their beliefs, thereby earning our admiration for their martyrdom. We need not accede to their beliefs in order to honor them — it is enough that they believed. It is commonly recognized that the truth of a belief is in no way necessary for the courage and sanctity of sacrifice. Yet, we also seem to revere a few, Socrates chiefly, who die, not for beliefs, and not for truths, but just for Truth itself. When analyzed, this usually means that Socrates or some other sacrificial philosopher has accepted death rather than surrender his passionate search for truth. Yet, this analysis scarcely leads us to relabel the sacrifice as a death for the *Search* for Truth. We insist Socrates died for Truth, and not merely for the search for truth. But even Socrates would never claim that all his judgments and beliefs were true. So again, the falseness of Socrates' beliefs does not keep us from asserting he died for truth, any more than the truth of the martyr's beliefs prohibits us from thinking of him as one who died for belief. We insist that the martyr died for his *beliefs* even if they were true, and that Socrates died for *truth* even if his beliefs were false. Yet this seems to raise a serious problem. For surely Socrates died because he lived a life of inquiry, not because the things he said were all true. We simply do not accept the latter claim, but we do accept the former claim. This becomes clearer when we recognize that *truth* (not the *true*) is itself questioning of the highest sort. Socrates, as questioner, dies not for questioning but for Truth because Truth is the loftiest kind of questioning. But in solving the minor puzzle of how Socrates can be said to have died for Truth, have we not uncovered a greater paradox? Surely we have lost all right to respect if we insist questions are more important—more true—than answers. If I ask "What is the cure for pneumonia?" what counts is not the question but the answer, "modern antibiotics." In this case the question represents the agony of uncertainty, the dread the child may die, the submission of one's helplessness before the ignorance of that which matters. The answer is relief and gratitude and lofty respect for the advance in medical science. So surely answers *are* superior to questions.

Of course they are. If one's interest is the solution to problems or the advance of knowledge, questions are merely the necessary steps taken to achieve the long-sought results: health, happiness, and longer lives. But as necessary and admirable as these things are, the present inquiry is about truth, not true answers. So it is imperative once again to return to the philosophical meaning of questioning as a resource for understanding what Truth means.

Let us assume this sentence is true: "The cat is on the mat." However, even as simple and straightforward as this harmless sentence appears it is not obvious what it means. Indeed, simply written there in its boldness it may have no meaning at all. Why would anyone *say* such a thing? Perhaps one might utter this sentence in response to a wife's uneasy question, "Honey, where's the cat?" The above sentence is now intelligible as information which locates. But a querulous neighbor might ask: "What on earth is that hideous grey thing on the mat?" The sentence in response to this question now identifies rather than locates. But the child, familiar with the antics of her pet, may also ask: "Is my cat on or under the mat?" Now the sentence functions as a decision procedure. But to locate, to identify, and to decide between alternatives are three entirely different acts, all communicated by the same sentence. Hence it is obvious that the sentence, by itself, is not meaningful—and hence cannot even be true—until we know the prior *questions* which prompt it. The sentence, as an answer, is incomplete without the prior question. After all, people don't usually go around suddenly saying totally irrelevant things which may happen to be accurate. Unless one is a dadaist or is practicing locution, sentences are supposed to occur in context, and this context can almost always be articulated in terms of a prior possible question. Thus the ability to question—which now means to go back from the accepted true sentence to find, not answers, but prior questions which must be assumed if the answer is to be intelligible—is indeed the realm of Truth.

The example of the cat on the mat, however, is meant only to show that answers are not independent of questions. This indicates the priority of questioning. But, when one speaks of living or dying for the truth one usually has in mind a concern for the lofty and great mysteries of existence. Philosophers ask about God and destiny and suffering and reality, not about cats on mats. These, we say, are the ultimate questions— the things that really matter.

But in speaking this way do we not expose the very paradox which is so devastating for the philosopher? We speak of the great questions, not the great answers. But surely the analysis of the above sentence about the cat on the mat has shown not merely that claims presuppose questions, but that questions in order to be rational and meaningful must permit of possible answers. Yet, the very idea of a philosopher providing a cessation to the inquiry is almost sacrilegious. Granted that Hegel writes in the Introduction to his *Phenomenology of Spirit* that he has replaced the love of knowledge with the possession of it, most readers either do not believe him or recognize that his understanding of knowledge is itself so singular that his claim does not threaten the inquisitorial or erotic nature of philosophy. So the paradox remains. The philosopher is a questioner, but of such ultimate questions he can expect no answers. But questions without answers are as suspect as answers without questions, and even if we admit the questioning may reveal to us a profounder understanding of what truth means, we still want to insist there are answers somewhere.

The paradox cannot be defanged by the mere tactic of asserting that such answers are more difficult to find than most, and that the miserable unsuccess of philosophers to find the truth they have been looking for must be accepted because of the lofty and troubling nature of the questions. The point is, there are many successful answers in the history of philosophy, but the answers are peculiarly dissatisfying, for though they do indeed offer a response, they also provoke more interrogation. The paradox of philosophy is not that there are no answers, but simply that the answers become deeper questions.

The paradox of truth, however, is not merely a conceptual puzzle which delights clever minds and fascinates the members of Mensa. In the existential agony of our own wonder this paradox looms as a source of genuine torment. For we, as members of the species mankind, are not in possession of infinite wisdom, or even of knowledge, especially of the great questions. Is God real or an illusion? Are we merely animals with no higher calling than gratification? Why do we exist? Why does morality matter? It seems we simply cannot know for certain the answers to any of these questions, and so we take refuge in our ignorance, and find satisfaction in belief. However, it is with the introduction of the dichotomy between belief and doubt that the agony of Truth becomes so wretched. For the more I *believe,* the less willing I am to allow I may be misguided—indeed there is a perverse arrogance found among many who would brazenly find virtue even in belief of what is false. ("I care not whether it is true; it is enough that I commit myself to it and believe. My salvation lies in belief, and so spectacular is my faith I will adhere to it even if it is shown to be contradictory and false.") Belief, therefore, seems to imply a suspension of the critical faculties and even an indifference to truth. Belief is therefore an enemy to truth. The more profoundly I believe, the less willing I am to question, and with the retreat of the questioning there is an inevitable shrinkage of the concern for Truth.

Cruelly, however, doubting is no closer friend to truth than belief. One of the easiest errors of thought to fall into is that of universal scepticism. The story is told of the great pre-Socratic critic, Cratylus, whose skillful success at speculating on possible objections to everything finally rendered him incapable of any belief whatsoever, so that he eventually ceased speaking, communicating, and socializing altogether, and was reduced to near zombielike passivity, apparently condescending only to wiggle his little finger as a gesture to his slave that he was hungry. The scepticism of Cratylus reaches beyond any and all reason for scepticism. If the critical in excess leaves one immobilized, it too is an enemy to truth. The ghost of Cratylus looms over the shoulder of every thinker as ominously as the ghost of the most implacable bigot. There can be no mistake about this agony—doubt is as inimical to truth as trust.

The difficulty lies in understanding where the boundaries of excess really are. When is it excessive to doubt and when is it excessive to believe? Is not every doubt inimical to truth, and every belief a retreat from truth? To admit I merely believe seems to imply a commitment in the absence of critical thinking, to doubt at all seems to place me on the slippery slope of Cratylean scepticism. But unless I doubt I have no critical resources, and unless I believe I am doomed to nihilism. If I trust in belief I am an enemy to truth; if I am so critical as to be a sceptic I am likewise an enemy to truth. Is truth, then, entirely uncritical disbelief? If so, truth is meaningless.

We seem to inherit this anguish of the paradox of truth along with our humanity. To be at all is to be tormented by this antinomy between doubt and trust. It does no good to appeal to moderation in such matters, for even if we were to be moderate, how would we ever know when our doubting is excessive or our believing naive? "Doubt one half of what you believe" is an appeal not to moderation but to silliness. Which half? And if I *consider* which half I can only do so critically, but that is not to believe at all, and Cratylus almost smiles at snagging another victim.

The torment of this anguish is so real many are persuaded to seek refuge in irrationality. Simply because misery loves company, more people seem willing to forgo their critical dubiety than their uncritical belief, but the lonely Cratylus and the accompanied bigot are equal strangers to Truth. It is the realization that this is so that makes the paradox of Truth so cruel.

Yet the paradox, as paradox, does not allow us the comforting refuge of either sceptic or bigot. For the threat in both cases is the same: a cessation of inquiry just because in both Truth is denied. The anguish must persist, but the nihilism in the two extremes is avoided simply because we can and do still inquire. In point of fact, the paradox merely serves as urgency to inquiry: we embrace Truth, even if unknown, rather than accept the nihilism inherent in both scepticism and bigotry. It is true I cannot inquire unless I doubt (critically); but it is also true that I cannot inquire unless I believe. *Credo ut intelligam.* The question is not *what* I should doubt and *what* I should believe, as if one could ever make such judgments beforehand. Rather it is a matter of the realization that the profoundest belief is already critical and the profoundest criticism is already trust.

An American, criticizing the Constitution, does not decide to *doubt* the right to a fair trial and *believe* in the freedom of the press. Rather, in recognizing that an irresponsible press threatens a defendant's right to assumed innocence, the critic, in affirming both, limits both. There is a bigot's naiveté in blindly assuming the press can print beyond libel; there is a Cratylean scepticism in assuming that forensic restraint denies press freedom altogether. The serious critic of the Constitution tests these conflicts in his mind not because he rejects their importance and worth but because he accepts them. Unless the patriotic critic recognizes the tension between a totally free press and the right to assumed innocence he will never appreciate the infinite richness of this citadel among political documents. He *must* wince as he recognizes the necessary restraint on free expression in order to ensure fairness to the accused; and he *must* wince when the pestiferous and ubiquitous press seems to threaten the right to privacy inherent in the doctrine of assumed innocence. It is because he cares about all three—the Constitution itself, the right of a free press, and the right to assumed innocence—that he embraces both highly critical attacks and deep reverence for the seemingly conflicting institutions. The criticism is trustful and the trust is critical. Thus, although the anguish of the paradox of truth is real and torturous, the Truth itself demands the paradox, and so again it seems inevitable: The paradox of Truth is the Truth in paradox.

PART TWO:
ESTABLISHING THE REALM

4
'True' and 'Truth'

It seems we ask in order to stop asking. To ask is to invite an answer which attenuates our interrogation. If we ask: "Is the door closed?" and receive the correct response "Yes, it is closed," we then no longer ask. Indeed it seems meaningless to ask beyond the correct reply, for we cannot wonder or be uncertain or doubt, once we have accepted the answer as true. True answers therefore terminate the questioning; indeed, the very question itself seems little more than an invitation to elicit the true response. At the very most, the question seems to reflect merely our ignorance of the matter and our desire to remedy that ignorance. Of course, one can always ask *other* questions—*who* closed the door?—but such questions are merely further instances of ignorance coupled with a desire to know what is the case. Once I have been told that the door is closed it makes no sense for me to continue questioning whether it is closed.

Yet, we seem to be able to wonder and inquire even about things that we know quite well to be the case. I may know perfectly well that this man is my friend, but the assurance of the fact in no way keeps me from wondering about what a friendship is. The very fact of the friendship may provoke in me a need to inquire further. Yet, the nature of this further inquisition is not readily obvious. It is easy to understand why I may want to know *whether* the door is closed or *whether* the man is my friend; but why would I inquire into the *meaning* of friendship if I am quite satisfied with the relationship? Raising the question of meaning in no way improves the friendship; the probing does not make me a better friend, nor does it provide me with insights that can be translated into practical benefits. But if this new kind of asking does not make us better friends, what can it do for the friendship? Perhaps nothing at all.

This objection must be respected and weighed. Why ask such questions if the probing yields no beneficial results? It is tempting—indeed almost irresistibly—to insist that such asking must improve the friendship if only to the extent that I will be a *wiser* friend. But this temptation, like all temptations, promises more than it provides. To be sure, these questions beyond the practical concerns are not empty or meaningless. Indeed, such questions alter the questioner greatly, but not *as friend* but *as inquirer*.

There is a further temptation to be resisted. By probing beyond the settled and accepted fact of our friendship to the meaning of such a relationship, it may be thought we can develop a deeper appreciation of being friends. But even though this may occur, it is neither the reason nor the justification for asking such questions. It is a common misconception that pleasures taken in the results of an endeavor are thereby properly understood as the motive or the reason for the endeavor. I may feel a certain amount of satisfaction in the performance of my duty, but it does not follow that this satisfaction is the reason for doing my duty. In the same way, any appreciation or satisfaction I may enjoy as a result of asking beyond the established fact cannot account for the asking itself.

What, then, are the changes wrought by this further asking? If asking about the meaning of friendship alters me not as friend but as inquirer, how are we to understand this alteration? One immediate change that reveals itself in an obvious way is the difference that occurs in the very status of questioning itself. For, unlike the question asking whether the door is closed, here the answer neither satisfies nor accounts for the questioning—indeed the very notion of an answer, so fundamental to the first kind of asking, plays no role at all in establishing the validity of the question. When we ask whether something is the case, the possibility of an attenuating and decisive answer seems a necessary condition for the legitimacy of the question. If someone asks whether the door is closed, we accept the question as meaningful and legitimate primarily because it can be positively answered one way or the other. If someone asks whether something is the case in a circumstance where no such answer is possible, we tend to doubt the legitimacy of the question itself. "How heavy is the color green?" cannot be answered, and thus the question itself is indicted. But in asking the question of what friendship means we do not assume that an attenuating and decisive answer will satisfy and justify the questioning. There must, of course, be a possible response; but the question now is the ground of the response, whereas in the first case the response was the ground of the question. In no way is this due to the complexity or depth of the question regarding meaning. Many questions of fact are remarkably complex and troubling in their depth. Rather, the two kinds of questions are fundamentally different in terms of the very way in which they are asked, and in which the asking is understandable. It seems clear that the fundamental presupposition for the legitimacy of the first kind of question — the question which asks whether something is the case — is the possibility of a true answer. In the second kind of question what must be presupposed in order to certify the question as legitimate is the possibility that the question opens up the Truth. And so for the sake of clarity it is possible to offer a formal distinction between the true and the truth. This offering is provisional and as yet imprecise. But what is of primary importance here and now is the realization that this distinction has its origin in the kinds of questions being asked. To ask whether or what kind or how is to assume a true answer; to ask for the meaning or essence is to approach the truth.

This distinction is not restricted to events or causes. Indeed, to explain the second kind of questioning as an inquiry into meaning is misleading, for the first kind of questioning, which is ruled by the notion of the true, also can concern itself with meaning, though in a different sense than the questioning which is governed by the truth.

I ask: what is a mother? The dictionary provides an answer: a female parent. The definition succeeds; there is no further need — indeed no further possibility — of asking.

And yet, knowing perfectly well that a mother is a female parent, we seem to be able to wonder and probe beyond this acceptable and correct identification. How do we think about what it means to be a mother? Mothers forgive their sons beyond all ethical limits; they give beyond what they have, and love beyond their own interests. A mother protects with stunning ferocity, and in her forgiving, loving, giving, and protecting the child becomes aware that he matters *as* her child. Unbounded forgiveness and inexhaustible service tell us what a mother *is*.

But not all mothers love and forgive; yet all mothers are female parents. The lexicographer is thereby established as the source of the true definition, because his descriptions cover all mothers, good and bad. But is an unloving, unforgiving mother a *true* mother? The lexicographer's definition is true, but does it define a true mother? A 'true mother' is not the same as a 'good mother'; for a good mother may realize that her instinct to forgive may have a bad educative effect on a troublesome child, and hence check it, recognizing that the punishment is not only deserved but instructive. Such a mother is both true and good. But the mother who, through misguided sympathy, forgives her unruly child too frequently and hence is not a good mother is nevertheless a true mother just because we understand her forgiveness by an appeal to her being a mother. When 'what it means to be a mother' explains her devotion we understand her as being a mother *in truth.* In order for there to be truth, we must understand not only what is true, but also what is understood in truth.

There is surely more to understand in a mother when we reflect on her awesome capacity to forgive and protect, but the difference between the true and the truth is not merely the substitution of one set of predicates for another. The reflection upon maternal forgiveness and love as the essence of a mother does not provide an answer; rather it provokes a question or even a series of questions. We not only recognize that mothers forgive, but are amazed by it, and since such forgiveness is often unwarranted, we are troubled by it. How are we to think about this? Should we condemn mothers for being too emotional? Should not the child be punished rather than forgiven? Where does this strength and affection come from? For when we locate the essence of motherhood in a willingness to forgive beyond justice it is difficult to revere and respect such actions. At the same time, even though maternal love is not always consistent with propriety, its power fills us with awe and wonder. We are forced to *think,* precisely because this deeper penetration provides a conflict. Essences, therefore, which are the realm of truth rather than the true, are always troubling rather than satisfying.

The example of a mother may mislead us into believing that only emotional or value-tainted notions can be thought in this way. But even the most value-neutral concept can be examined on the levels of the true and truth, with the latter always resulting in a provocation of troubled reflection. It is possible to define matter (as Descartes does) by saying it takes up space. This purports to be a true definition, and if we accept it the questioning is terminated and no further inquiry is necessary. But if we probe from the true to the truth, from the definition which tells us *what* it is or the decision which informs us *whether* it is, to the essence which shows us what it means, we confront one of the great paradoxes of the philosophical mind. Granted matter takes up space, but how much space is necessary for a thing to qualify as matter? Is there a tiniest particle? No matter how tiny we imagine the particle to be, we can also imagine it being divided further. And so the question of the nature of space, whether it is ultimately divisible or finally indivisible, reveals the fundamental way we *must* think about matter. We thus understand the essence of matter as a profound question which, again, is not grounded in a determinant answer. But questions seem by their very nature to be indeterminate and relative. It would seem that one can ask any question one likes or happens to be bothered with at a given time. Only answers reveal knowledge, and hence asking seems an entirely arbitrary endeavor. How can questions, which manifest only our ignorance and hence are indefinite, provide us with a deeper understanding of the essence of anything, from space to mothers?

Of course, not just any question will serve. In the above example, the question itself is just as precise and revealing as any answer. Asking whether matter or space is infinitely divisible focuses our thinking in a more exact way than any other question about matter, such as where it comes from or what properties and characteristics it may have. In this higher sense, when the focus is on truth rather than what is true, a question is less a statement of ignorance coupled with a desire to know than a beacon which guides us to the narrow opening of our journey. The question functions as a source of illumination, precisely because on this level, to ask is to probe, and to probe is to advance.

False questioning, therefore, becomes a far greater danger in the realm of *truth* than false answers; though to be sure, in the realm of the *true* it is the other way around. To question, in the realm of truth, is not to ask for knowledge, because I already know. I know what mothers are and I know what space is. What asking does when I go beyond such knowing is to guide my thinking toward the essence or meaning, that is, the *thinkability* of such notions. But if this is the case, then false steps consist not in erroneous claims or improper answers but in false questioning. The procedure of success in the search for essential meaning will therefore be marked by a series of refined questions. "That is not the proper question; ask rather this..." or: "This formulation of the questioning is misleading; the asking should rather proceed along the following lines..." In other words, we question in order to learn, but we learn in order to question. To be able to question properly just is the gift of the greatest philosophers. All the advances in human wisdom (not 'science') turn on the asking of remarkably new and revealing questions. Of course, only those deeply involved in the study of such matters could even raise a genuinely profound question, for the *asking* itself is an essential part of what it means to be wise.

The realization that mothers forgive beyond what justice permits and the awareness that space must but cannot be infinitely divisible are not merely puzzles which confound ready analysis. We are amazed by both of these notions; the mind, unless it is numbed by indifference, wonders at these frustrations of its own rules. Yet, it is rarely appreciated that what makes us wonder and what causes us to be amazed is that these beckonings to further thought are precisely what reveals truth. We are stunned by the bottomless forgiveness of mothers precisely because we realize that such troubling notions somehow reveal to us how we must think if we are to understand what it means for there to be mothers. The unresolvable paradox of ultimate divisibility reveals how we must think if we are to approach the deepest meaning of space. Thus, it is not merely the conflict or puzzle which reveals truth, but also the awe and wonder that accompanies our realization of these ever elusive notions.

The distinction between the true and truth relies in part, though not entirely, on our ability to distinguish between questions that provoke terminal answers and those that uncover a profounder kind of wonder that results from our consideration of meaning. This difference is not the result of everyday language usage, as if we always used the word 'truth' to mean a lofty questioning of essences and the word 'true' to mean that determined by answers. The distinction is far more fundamental than that. On the other hand, neither does this distinction in any way suggest that truth is less objective, that our emotions and passions, being variant and relative, render truth somehow subjective. The terms 'true' and 'truth' both fundamentally resist arbitrary or relativistic significance. The two terms, after all, are but variants of a central meaning.

From the very beginning of philosophy a distinction of this sort—though not described as the true/truth distinction—has been assumed or utilized by the master thinkers, but in no texts quite as effectively as in Plato's dialogues. The argumentation in the *Laches* reveals this distinction with the seemingly effortless skill that Socrates always shows in his discussions. Laches is a skilled general who knows perfectly well what courage is: he knows how to spot it among his soldiers, he knows how to encourage his men to achieve it, and he knows its value on the battlefield. It is simply ridiculous to assume that the warrior Laches, who comes to Socrates to discover the best way to educate his sons, is unfamiliar with the virtue of courage. That he understands it well enough is evidenced in the first definition he gives to Socrates: "He is a man of courage who does not run away, but remains at his post and fights against the enemy" (191D; trans. Jowett). This is a vivid and helpful description, and in many ways actually tells us more about courage than the contorted analyses Socrates himself offers a few paragraphs later. Socrates then begins his usual refinement in which an overly narrow definition is broadened so as to be more universal. He points out that there are cases in which strategic withdrawal is obviously an act of courage, so that perhaps 'staying at one's post' may be misleading, a refinement to which Laches readily agrees. Unfortunately many commentators have seen in these lexicographical tunings the central contributions of the dialogue, which is absurd. It should be noted that Laches' first suggestion is an excellent candidate for a definition, and if the phrase 'staying at one's post' is taken somewhat liberally or even metaphorically as meaning 'fulfilling one's assigned duties', the definition would be acceptable even to a critical lexicographer.

Laches is invited to offer an even better definition, which he promptly does: "Courage is a sort of endurance of the soul" (192C). Again the reader can see by this that Laches knows perfectly well what courage is, and is not inept at expressing himself. This second response shows he has thought about courage and has directed his fine mind not merely to describing it, which he does fairly well in his first attempt, but actually to isolating its essential meaning. If for 'endurance' we might put 'steadfastness,' the suggestion is by no means an unworthy one.

Socrates again persists in challenging this account, but no longer is he merely trying to broaden an overly narrow description. He asks whether all endurance is noble, and whether before one can have courage—or *any* virtue for that matter—one must have wisdom. This questioning deepens the inquiry remarkably, for now Socrates is ready to show exactly where the problem lies. He asks: if two men, one sophisticated and one fairly inexperienced in warfare, were to go into battle, which would be more courageous? Laches responds that the greener youth would have more courage.

But of course, that is precisely the paradox. Surely the green recruit, terrified and uncertain of the impending danger, *is* more courageous than the seasoned veteran whose skill and experience fills him with confidence. Anyone who knows anything about human nature knows how much more courage it takes to confront not only an external enemy but the one within, the trembling, untried spirit of an uncertain soul. Yet, this very *question* completely alters the kind of thinking which precedes it. We are no longer trying merely to find a broad enough definition, we are now struggling with the very paradox of courage that forces us to *think* about it. The possibility of failure, the fear of *not* staying at one's post, turns out to be the very stuff and spirit of courage. Yet, if courage is noble—which it surely is—then it would seem we must admit that ignorance and fear are necessary for nobility. Like our realizations that mothers forgive beyond justice and that space must but cannot be infinitely divided, this discovery stuns us into a most profound realization. We now must think on an altogether different and indeed higher plane. For we are now no longer interested in merely discovering what courage *is*—Laches has shown us that right away. Rather, we are asking, not about the courageous youth, but about our own thinking. How do we *think* about courage? Why, by contrasting ignorance with wisdom, by recognizing that courage, as a *human* virtue, must comply with the human situation. A god, knowing all, can have no courage. The very torment between asking and wisdom is the struggle that is courage. We are confronting the essence of the virtue; we are considering the *truth* about courage.

In shifting from Laches' two perfectly acceptable definitions to Socrates' confrontation with the essence of courage, the dialogue directs our attention from what is true to the truth. This example is offered not as a resource for understanding Plato but simply to assist us in understanding why we must make some kind of distinction in order to understand the difference between these two approaches.

In the case of the mother we have seen that even though it is perfectly *true* to identify a mother as a female parent, that is not how we understand the meaning of a mother in *truth,* and so the true/truth distinction is offered to clarify and name the distinction. In the case of Plato's dialogue we see that whereas Laches is quite capable of giving us true descriptions, the philosopher Socrates is concerned with Truth. In both cases, however, we saw further that (1) truth seems to entail a kind of questioning which cannot be accounted for merely by reference to the attenuating answer, and that (2) the inquiry into truth seems almost always to assume some kind of 'essence'. And finally, we have seen that (3) the inquiry into essence or 'truth' is not carried out for practical or utilitarian purposes: the inquiry into the essence of friendship does not necessarily make me a better friend. (This point may be more intuitively obvious in the case of, say, competition; understanding the essence of competition would not make me a better competitor.)

Is the philosopher, therefore, the only one who seeks out 'truth', whereas all other disciplines are concerned with what is 'true'? This may be too strong a claim. But it is not too strong to suggest that only those concerned with confronting the 'essence' of a thing can be said to be concerned with the 'truth'. And so it seems inevitable that we now should direct our inquiry to the role of 'essence' in the search for the meaning of truth.

5
Truth and Essence

Arthur Schopenhauer, in Book III (§34) of *The World as Will and Representation,* writes: "Raised up by the power of the mind, we relinquish the ordinary way of considering things, and . . . no longer consider the where, the when, the why, and the whither in things, but simply and solely the What." The thinker and poet, he says later (§37), "know the *essential* in things which lies outside all relations" (trans. Payne). Thus, the pinnacle of thought and art is to achieve a direct confrontation with *what* something is—with its essence. Martin Heidegger, in his essay "The Origin of the Art-Work," writes: "What does the essential essence of something consist in? Presumably it lies in what the entity *is* in truth" (trans. Hofstadter). For both Schopenhauer and Heidegger, then, truth can be found only in the essences of things; truth is about 'essence', and thus 'essence' is, as Schopenhauer puts it, beyond "the ordinary way of considering things." Plato, too, in his famous depiction of the philosopher in the myth of the cave in the *Republic,* removes this concern for truth from ordinary concerns. The philosopher, defined as one who loves truth for its own sake, is precisely the one who has removed himself from the ordinary society within the cave and struggled to extricate himself from its concerns in order to comprehend directly the essence or form of things in truth.

Three entirely different thinkers, from entirely different epochs, with entirely different philosophical visions, nevertheless uniting in this one important realization: truth is the rare and extra-ordinary confrontation of essence. Why should truth be found only in the essential 'what'? And why, even if this is so, should truth be reserved for the few? One might understand Plato, as an aristocrat, maintaining such a thing, but both Schopenhauer and Heidegger are modern thinkers, living after the great antiaristocratic revolutions. Yet all three thinkers seem to link these two ideas—the elitism and the essentialism of truth. How are we to understand them?

Perhaps the elitism is merely one of sheer infrequency. Like chastity or sanctity, perhaps truth is simply too difficult for most to achieve. Or perhaps it is similar to talent or genius: few people can write like Shakespeare or compose like Beethoven, so perhaps only a few can achieve the necessary effort to confront pure essence, and so it is a rarity. If this is what is meant, it is a mere empirical observation, one which may be true but need not be true. It is even possible that the mere infrequency of achieving truth is due, not to a lack of intelligence or sensitivity, but simply to indifference. Most people do not achieve an understanding of essence, and hence of truth, simply because it is not as important or as interesting as other concerns. Perhaps the elitism is even more base: it may be due to a perversion of the mind, a kind of handicap like being born with a club foot. That truth is reserved for the few, or for moments of rarity, seems then an inessential and contingent matter, unworthy of being characterized.

All three thinkers, however, analyze the elitism inherent in the search for truth in far deeper terms. In the first place, the elitism implied in these analyses is not one of mere numerical infrequency. Whether it is a demographic fact that only a tiny percentage of the population is capable of grasping essential truth is an unworthy consideration, except as a warning that the methodology of achieving truth cannot be that of the pollster. Sociological surveys of how people "feel" about the truth are happily irrelevant. Rather, the notion of elitism in the search for truth is conceptual. Schopenhauer put it best: essential truth is achieved only when we "relinquish the ordinary way of considering things." Hence it is not only extraordinary people who think about essence, but people who think in an extraordinary way. It may be a contingent fact that *only* extraordinary people do indeed think in an extraordinary way, but such a fact need not be inevitable and hence is unimportant. What *is* important is that one must recognize that there are both ordinary and extraordinary ways of thinking, and Plato, Heidegger, and Schopenhauer have all taken great care in explaining just what that difference is. In this conceptual sense, then, the elitism of philosophy is indeed essential and even helpful in illuminating what the rarified meaning of truth must be.

What, then, is the difference between "ordinary thinking" and "extraordinary thinking"? Schopenhauer's analysis is probably the clearest: by ordinary thinking he means thinking in accordance with the principle of sufficient reason, that is, thinking in terms of space, time, cause, and purpose. It is the kind of thinking we do in order to solve problems, to make sense of events, and to bring about satisfaction of our wants. On the other hand, for Schopenhauer, extraordinary thinking, which focuses solely on the essence or the 'what', must abandon the principle of sufficient reason and contemplate nothing but the sheer meaning. The difference between Laches' true definition of courage and Socrates' philosophical understanding of courage in Truth already provides us with at least a vague sense of what this might mean.

But why 'essence'? Even if we grant there should be a distinction between 'true' and 'truth,' or between Schopenhauer's "ordinary" thinking and the "extraordinary" thinking of the philosopher, why should this 'truth' or this "extraordinary thinking" have anything to do with essences? Why not simply with things, or reality, or relations?

The seeming familiarity with notions evidenced in our ability to use terms properly and meaningfully has provoked some thinkers, particularly Ludwig Wittgenstein, to deny there is any essence. Rather, these thinkers object, the proper meaning of any term just is its proper usage. There is no deep or mysterious meaning to philosophical notions, and proper philosophical analysis consists in therapeutically removing from us any need to search beyond what is obvious in our everyday language. Romeo loves Juliet, and most of us know exactly what this means. We can spot the obvious evidence of how they feel for each other in their behavior, and since both they and we use the term correctly, it is obvious that "love" is not a great *question* at all because, in fact, we already know perfectly well what it means. There is, to be sure, a problem when one tries to define love or isolate the essence of love; but this is due, not to the inherent ineffability of love, but to the illusory notion that there are essences at all. We are quite familiar with love because we can recognize it in the world, feel it as an emotion within ourselves, or use the term correctly. But we cannot grasp the essence of love or anything else because one cannot grasp what does not exist. "Essence" is nothing but an ephemeral vagueness which results from confusing an abstraction with what is concrete. Or it is the result of the fallacy of reifying what is purely mental. To sigh or pine achingly for some mysterious "essence" of love is a form of philosophical neurosis—or in basket cases like Socrates in the *Clouds,* perhaps even psychosis—which must simply be purged by therapy, that is, the proper analysis of terms.

Since truth seems nothing more than an abstraction from various instances of true propositions, and since we obviously do know how to use the term 'true', there can be nothing mysterious about it, and hence where we thought there was a great problem or question there turns out to be nothing more than the common event known as abstract generalization. The Truth is whatever is common to the various particular true events or true sentences, and can therefore be of little interest to the thinker beyond these therapeutic refinements. Similarly, the medieval notion of "essence" ceases to be compelling just because there is no such thing. Rather, the different uses of a term display a family resemblance. As a consequence there is no *essence* of truth, since, strictly speaking, essence has been replaced by family resemblances and truth has been understood as an abstraction.

This intriguing analysis may seem attractive, especially in light of the previous chapters. In one painless reanalysis we remove all agony of paradox and submit to whatever therapies are required to keep us from asking meaningless questions. For it is important to all thinkers not to yield to the temptation of wallowing in verbal wonderlands precisely because they are illusory.

What, after all, could we possibly *want* to understand about truth beyond our ability to use the term properly and to identify those who have that ability and those who do not? What do we reach for beyond the proper usage of any term whatsoever? Are not the Wittgensteinians correct in their claim that philosophers who seek for essence or ultimate definitions are simply epistemic neurotics—searching for things that simply are not there? Like the schizophrenic who hears threats in ordinary conversation, do not the philosophers hear strange voices beckoning them to some mysterious depth beyond the grasp of ordinary mortals? An artist who claims he loves beauty simply means that he appreciates this beautiful woman, that beautiful mountain, these beautiful children. But the philosopher who claims he loves truth apparently does not mean he loves this true proposition, that true claim, or these true judgments. What is there to love in the true claim that ink stains? It is *true*. But, since such truths are unworthy of love or even of dutiful concern, the philosopher must somehow persuade us that the Truth is a deep and mysterious matter, when all it is is an abstraction from various truths which are known and some, but not most, of which may be interesting.

Consider the reaction young parents often display at the arrival of their first child. They wax eloquent at the miracle of childbirth, express awe at the mystery of life, and protest gratitude for this gift of a human infant which is now wondrously their own. But we know there is nothing mysterious at all, nor, given the frequency of its occurrence, much to wonder at. We know all the causes, all the medical explanations, all the rules and odds and predictions, and so it is *not* a miracle. We even know that this sense of wonder will soon transmogrify into weary acceptance. What the youthful parents mean by their use of 'miracle' and 'wonder' is simply their unexpected emotion thrilling them by its newness. Their devotion to their child is a natural phenomenon, built into us as an instinct for the preservation of the species. Their appeal to wonder, miracle, and mystery is simply a manifestation of their own inexperience and the impoverishment of their vocabulary.

But at least the young parents know their child is real. The child conjured by the philosopher—the essence—is ephemeral. It does not even cry at night or wet the diapers.

I look at the watch upon my wrist and note the hour. My use of the term 'watch' is proper. I know how to use the watch, how to make it work, its cost, its reliability. If pressed, I may even read about the history of watches and how they came to be so curiously divided into twelve units. But aside from these purely practical matters is there anything else to understand about a watch? There may be some verbal refinements I must use if I am hired to write a dictionary, but the skill in denoting is not extraordinary. I may first define a watch as a humanly created instrument, small enough to wear on the wrist or carry in a small pocket, designed to keep and measure time by means of hands pointing at twelve numbers arranged in a circle. But then one might point out the occurrence of digital watches and thus require a refinement. There is simply nothing else to know or understand. The definition of a watch should be broad enough to include the variants and narrow enough to exclude the larger clocks, but there is no *essence,* no existing single referent of all the uses of the term. What else is there except the actual, common, nonmysterious, functional things in space and time called watches? There is also the abstract general concept 'watch' which does not itself tell time; but we understand how concepts work in language. Thus there is no truth or essence in watches. There are true claims made about watches but no essential truth to the idea 'watch'. How are we to make sense of this Wittgensteinian critique? The point is, if by 'essence' we mean a covering definition, then Wittgenstein is probably correct.

Or if we mean by the term some metaphysical property or predicate, then too he is probably correct.

But is not this "ordinary language" critique precisely limited in the very way which the essentialist desires to transcend? To be sure, we may learn a great deal from an analysis of ordinary language usage, but if the argument is made that essentialist understanding is by definition *not* ordinary, then has not the critique entirely missed the point? Schopenhauer describes essence in terms which go beyond ordinary language; to protest that an analysis of ordinary language will not reveal essence is not so much a critique as an admission that ordinary language is merely limited. What the critique would have to accomplish would be to show that ordinary language is all we have, that any appeal beyond it is also beyond all reason and human possibility; and *that* claim cannot be proven merely by an *appeal* to common language, for such an argument begs the question.

What *is* essence? The three philosophers cited above agree that truth is of essence, and that such truth is reserved for the few or at least the extraordinary, but they seem to disagree about what is meant by essence. For Schopenhauer, essence is that which can be known only by avoiding the principle of sufficient reason, when the mind concerns itself solely with the 'whatness' of a thing. For Heidegger, essence is achieved only when one questions in the light of the ontological meaning of Being. For Plato, essence is the *eidos* or 'thinkability' of a thing—the "form." Which of these three thinkers provides the keenest insight into what essence means? Or is it possible to describe essence in such a way as to incorporate the fundamental thinking of all three in spite of their obvious differences? This can be done if great care is taken in the approach, for although the three philosophers obviously have different understandings of essence, their basic insights are sufficiently similar to allow an analysis which will at least answer their chief concerns.

When I hear a siren, I know I should get out of the way; when I hear the telephone ring, I know I should pick up the receiver. These are occasions in "ordinary existence" in which hearing something entails a call to action. It is not the telephone or siren itself, but rather how I hear them—as evocations to certain actions—that makes such events intelligible. How would it be possible to focus solely on hearing itself? Suppose I hear a symphony or a sonnet. In these cases I am *not* provoked to further action; I am content to listen. The art form, therefore, lets hearing be meaningful just by itself. Music and poetry provide me with the essence of hearing, because I do not hear *in order to do something else*, I simply enjoy hearing. Indeed, in cases where the music is exceptionally fine or the poetry especially profound, I may realize, in these experiences, just what it means to be able to hear at all. The rupture of the hearing experience from its ordinary role of informing, warning, announcing, and so on, and its elevation to the extraordinary one of simply hearing for its own sake provides me with an understanding of what it means to hear, and that is its essence.

A shift in the choice of the art may be helpful. Suppose I enter a building in order to get out of the rain, or to do a particular thing, such as entering a restaurant in order to have dinner. In these two cases the building is a means to something else. But the art of architecture may inspire me to enter a building simply to discover what it means to dwell. Dwelling is a mode of existence, and a great architect will so design his building as to make dwelling meaningful. Indeed, entering a beautiful building may awaken in me for the first time an awareness of the importance and significance of dwelling. The building, then, as a work of art, reveals what it means to be a dwelling being. The practical and utilitarian functions of a building, such as keeping me warm and dry and providing a place for the furniture, which allow me to do other things such as sitting down or bathing or dining or achieving privacy are all submerged into secondary concerns when the artistry of the architect succeeds in revealing to me the simple but astonishing essence of dwelling. And of course a moment's reflection will reveal that this is precisely what great architects do indeed achieve. Their art, then, though doubtless providing the ordinary services of keeping me warm and dry, also reveals something of great importance about my own existence—namely, that dwelling matters *just by itself.* The truth or essence of dwelling is thus revealed by the artistry of the architect.

We might say that a magnificent building tells us how to think about what it means to dwell. But it is the architect whose business it is to reveal the essence of dwelling; it is the philosopher whose business it is to tell us the essence of thinking. Thus, artist and thinker both reveal essence, though in different ways. Obviously nonthinkers cannot dwell, though they may certainly enter into and use buildings; but conversely, nondwellers cannot think, though they may certainly know what a building is for.

To hear a symphony or to dwell in a beautiful building is to confront the essence of hearing and dwelling. This means that, in dwelling, I need not explain my being in the building by appealing to anything else. In hearing the symphony I need not *explain* my listening by appealing to anything else except the sheer delight I take in *hearing* it. Therefore, the most philosophically significant attribute of essence is its independence in terms of explanation. To grasp the essence of something is to apprehend its meaning without external explanation. To understand essence is therefore to achieve that status of comprehension which needs no further account. When the true mother forgives her son, what *explains* this action is simply her being a mother. If I ask: "Why did that woman forgive that boy?" the response, "Because she is his mother," not only explains the act, it itself needs no further explanation. I do not need to explain my hearing the symphony beyond what it reveals to me about what it means to hear. Essence, then, explains meaning but cannot itself *be* explained by elements outside itself. In essence the series of explanations ceases.

This reflection on the nature of essence reveals the first fundamental attribute of Truth. Truth is ultimate. By this is meant that the essence of something is the source of explaining it, and itself need not, or perhaps even cannot, be further explained. I can ask: "Why did you enter this building?" and be answered, "To get out of the rain." But, if the building, as a piece of great architecture, reveals what it means to dwell, I cannot ask, "Why do you dwell?" but can only ask, "What does it mean to dwell?" However, it is the genius of the architect that reveals this meaning (or 'essence') through his art.

We do not first dwell and then find architects to provide us with buildings in which we can dwell. Rather, it is only through architecture that we can dwell at all. Architecture is the source of the *essence* of dwelling.

The analysis of these examples reveals a notion of essence which is consistent with the contributions of Plato, Schopenhauer, and Heidegger. From Plato's account of the *eidos* we learn that essence must provide us with how we think about a thing—that is, essence is the concrete idealization of what makes a thing able to be thought. From Schopenhauer we learn that essence cannot be approached through causal or purposive thinking, and from Heidegger we learn that questioning about essence must always be formulated in terms of what it means to be.

Thus we do not ask what the essence of a building is, as Schopenhauer and Plato might, but what it means to dwell in buildings. We might ask what a mother *is,* but the existential essence would be how we *think* about mothers, which satisfies Plato's chief concern. Both Schopenhauer and Heidegger have argued in slightly different ways that art is a source of truth, and the examples have shown how the artist succeeds in revealing the essence of certain modalities, such as dwelling, hearing, and being a mother. If care is taken to formulate the meaning of essence in *existential* terms—and by this is meant that the notion is always formulated in terms of what it means to *exist* in such and such a way, as hearer or dweller or parent—then the "ordinary language" critique can be avoided. For essence is not a metaphysical property somehow "in" the object, nor is it a linguistic covering term.

This analysis has revealed a genuinely fundamental insight about truth as essence, that as the source of how we *think* about something, the existential essence reveals the truth as ultimate. When 'being a mother' *explains* behavior which otherwise would be unintelligible, we recognize that the truth or essence of being a mother is not further explained by something else. This crucial, indeed *critical,* discovery now needs a thorough examination.

6
Truth as Ultimate

In the *Critique of Pure Reason* Kant argues that reason always seeks for the unconditioned. The mind is ever restless in its probing until it can find some sort of terminus or satisfaction. In what Schopenhauer calls "ordinary thinking" this terminus is an answer. The distinction between the true and truth allows us to identify the true answer as that which gives *knowledge,* and knowledge is the terminus of ordinary thinking. But just as a true answer attenuates ordinary questions, so in the realm of truth some resting place must be found for the inquirer. Essence seems to provide this terminus, and in the higher realm of questioning we discover that truth has the peculiarity that as essence, it is ultimate. We have seen in the previous chapter that because essence illuminates or explains, there can be no further inquisition beyond it. The essential truth of what a mother is explains her behavior. Yet, an essence does not terminate inquiry in the same way that true answers terminate legitimate questions, for although being a mother may explain why she forgives her son, and hence we can no longer ask *why* she forgives or even why she is a mother, we can and do continue to wonder what it *means to be* a mother. So, although essence quite properly is the realm of truth, and to that extent is ultimate, the ability to continue to probe and wonder lies still within it. Essence does not attenuate inquiry—rather it *encloses* it, provides it with its possibility. But, as ultimate, essence provides the only response which satisfies the need for what Kant calls the unconditioned.

When we speak of the search for truth, then, the terminus or essence must provide the search with sufficient weight and promise to make the asking intelligible. For it would not be at all rational if the asking of these questions were merely an unending series of ever more frustrating interrogations. When we seek the truth, after all, what is sought is that which would make the seeking worthwhile. When asked what sadness lengthens his hours, Romeo replies: "Not having that, which having, makes them short." And so it is with truth: we long for that, which having, would make us long no longer. But in the previous discussion we saw that truth, unlike true answers, provokes not only further questions but different *kinds* of questions. I may ask: why does this woman scrub the floors at night? To which one answers, "To make extra money?" "Why does she want or need it?" "To get her undeserving son out of jail." "But why does she do that?" "Because she is his mother." At this point it would be absurd to ask: "Why is she his mother?" And so in *this* sense the series of whys must cease. But the asking now becomes a matter of truth rather than knowledge (true answers) when we seek to understand this by asking: "What does it mean to be a mother?" Delving into this question may well provoke wonder and awe, and hence provide even more questioning, but the realm of the question—the essence of motherhood—remains the ultimate resource for intelligibility. We are assured that however more deeply we probe, or whatever further questions arise, they will be within the realm of, and about, the essence of motherhood, and to this extent essence is indeed ultimate. For by 'ultimate' is meant merely the end of the series of whys—that is, Kant's unconditioned.

To say that truth is ultimate is therefore not to predicate of truth some synthetic addendum, for being ultimate in the sense of ending the series of whys is what is *meant* by truth. In a paraphrase of Romeo's famous response, we ask after that which, in having, would end our asking. It makes no sense to seek that which is already found. The detective does not continue to look for clues which would identify the culprit once the guilty has been discovered and his identity proved. The detective searches for the truth, finds it, and the search is over. So "ending the search" is part of what truth means.

If this point seems belabored, it is because the significance of it is too often overlooked. In truth we confront the ultimate. Indeed, 'to be in truth' is 'to be in the face of the ultimate'. The obviousness of this in no way relieves us of the need to examine what it means. What does it mean to confront the ultimate?

It might seem that any time we reach that point in our analysis at which we stop asking 'why' and start wondering about what it means to be something, we confront the ultimate, and so there is nothing special about it. But the question we are now raising concerns what it means to exist in truth—or to be more precise, what it means to exist such that the confrontation with the ultimate is rendered open to inquiry. We want to know what it is like to be in truth, and that just means what it is like to confront that which cannot be explained by reference to any more whys. But the locution 'what it is like' is merely unrefined, everyday jargon. The proper terminology would be to raise the question in terms of existential phenomena which reveal what it means to confront the truth. How, in other words, can we confront the truth? What is it about us that provides the possibility of confronting or facing truth as ultimate essence? Are there indeed certain existential phenomena, that is, ways in which we exist, that reveal this special sense of confronting the ultimate? If we ask this question properly, we may find the following four encounters peculiarly well suited for analysis.

1. I see a man working, and since he seems not to enjoy his labor, I ask him why. To make extra money, he says. Why do you want extra money, that you should labor so hard? Because, he says, I want to buy a boat. Why do you want to buy a boat? Because I like to sail; I get pleasure out of sailing.

Can I ask *now:* why do you take pleasure? Or is it the case that pleasure is a rather unique notion, in that it seems to explain itself? Aristotle argues in the *Nicomachean Ethics* that pleasure is an *intrinsic* good, and by that he means that pleasure cannot or need not be explained by reference to anything else. The brief description of the conversation with the laborer reveals this to be the case. I do not need to explain beyond pleasure; my taking pleasure in something is sufficient to account for why I do it. To be sure, at times I may take pleasure immorally, and in such cases the pleasure is not justified; but even when it is immoral, pleasure explains. Not only does it explain, it itself cannot be explained by anything more fundamental. It may be good to have pleasure, at least under certain conditions, but even so the goodness does not explain the pleasure. I do not take pleasure because it is good but because it pleases. Thus, in pleasure I confront an ultimate way of existing, if by ultimate is meant that no higher level of explanation is needed. Pleasure is ultimate.

2. A decent, intelligent, hard-working young woman is suddenly stricken with a painful and total paralysis. Her unscrupulous husband abandons her, taking their children away, leaving her immobilized and inarticulate in a public ward, meagerly cared for by strangers, and in constant pain. Her mind is still alert and active, confronting her with the daily and cruel question of why she should be so wretchedly

unfortunate. She deserves better. The anguished "Why me?" that can be read in her mute but pleading eyes is not a plaintive whimper but an authentic demand. Why me, indeed. Her suffering is admittedly undeserved and cruel; but need it also be nihilistic? Can it be thought about? Is there a divine providence that supplies some cosmic justification for her plight? But if she is deprived of knowing this, then is her fate not all the more unacceptable? And if, in despair, she desires suicide but cannot accomplish it unassisted, are we bound by her desire to make such dreadful judgment?

We cannot answer her question, "Why me?" It is, we say, her fate. There is a certain authenticity in recognizing that her question simply cannot be answered. *At all.* Indeed, any attempt to explain to her *why* she is fated is an insult to the dignity and enormity of her suffering. To say "it will make you stronger" is an outrage; to say "God wills it" says nothing, since it admits the explanation is beyond human comprehension. To say "it is fate" does not explain, either; for fate is not a cause or a responsible agent. Yet, in a curious sense, we all must admit that our fate is indeed a part of our existence. Whether we like it or not, we are beings who do not control all, or even most, of what goes on to make us who we are. So, on the one hand, if we appeal to fate as some kind of explanatory force we are grossly mistaken about how concepts explain; but if we deny that our fate is indeed an essential part of who we are, we are likewise grossly mistaken, and existentially beguiled. So, how are we to *think* about fate? We cannot deny we *are* fated, yet we cannot appeal to fate as a source of understanding or intelligibility. Fate, therefore, is also ultimate. It is ultimate in an entirely different way than pleasure, but it is ultimate nonetheless. To confront fate—which we really cannot avoid, though we can deceive ourselves into pretending we can avoid it—is therefore to confront the ultimate.

3. Knowing full well that it was improper and wrong, he nevertheless yielded to the self-indulgent allure of his own comfort and deceit, and lied about his promise, deeply offending her. As a result she suffered unwarranted pain and humiliation. There was no doubt the fault was entirely his, and as the consequences of his selfish cruelty became more and more obvious, the burden of his guilt first struck, and then settled onerously as the full weight pressed down on him with unmitigated accusation. He was guilty and he knew it. It was an offense not only against her but against their marriage, which was forever altered, and he alone was to blame. There was no extenuation, and were he to try to

excuse it with lame appeals, the burden could only increase. Why had he done it? How could he explain, even to himself, his responsibility? Were there causes that could account for it? Were there reasons to which he could appeal that would ease the burden, lighten the load? Of course, he knew he *could* appeal to reasons that might deflect the full burden of censure, but the solace and comfort they might offer were but further deceits. To distract this singular pressure of responsibility by begging even further untruths became unacceptable, for it would weigh even more heavily. He could not, and finally even would not, deny his burden. He was guilty.

Guilt seeks no further explanation. For indeed, as in the case of pleasure and fate, to explain it is to explain it away. In being guilty we simply must accept the fault as our own. There is no need to invent some entity which we might call a will, for that is to engage in metaphysical speculation, which cannot be assured. To be guilty is to be real in itself; there is no need to explain it even by metaphysics. It cannot be explained; rather guilt explains both the burden and the violation of what ought to be but is not. Guilt is ultimate.

In saying this the reference is not to the *feelings* that result from doing what is wrong. It is *being* guilty that matters, and what makes guilt real is precisely the acceptance of it as unexplained by any other condition or thing. It is primordial, in that there is no other being, no other cause, no other appeal except myself. To deny the guilt is to deny myself; to explain it by extenuating and alien forces is to cease to matter as a person. To be is to be guilty. It is a highly disturbing truth, but implacable in its demands. Guilt confronts us with the ultimate—again in a way totally unlike the confrontations found in pleasure or in fate. But like these two, the essentially ultimate nature of guilt simply cannot be avoided. In one sense it is the complete opposite of fate; for in the latter what oppresses is precisely our lack of control, but in guilt it is strangely but powerfully our own. Since neither can be escaped, though both are ours in perfectly diametrical senses, both confront us with the ultimate.

4. *Verweile doch! Du bist so schön!* Of course, he really did not believe it. The bargain, he thought, was a good one. The sinister visitor with the strange but wonderful powers would never be able to make him say that. But he knew, and we know as we hear him say it, that if there is anything which could make a man surrender his soul, it would be beauty. Surely no mere pleasure or adventure or any other satisfaction, not even knowledge itself, could bring the learned Faust to such abject capitula-

tion. Beauty alone disarms completely. It is the fundamental stop sign that brings all traffic to a halt. And so the cynical Faust doubts that Mephistopheles can produce a moment so beautiful as to arrest the tireless energy and eternal longing of his spirit. At the same time the very suggestion that there *might* be something that is simply *too* beautiful finally breaks all of Faust's last scruples, for beauty alone seems worthy of worship and sacrifice, even the sacrifice of one's soul.

But Goethe's drama is not mere fantasy. Most of us are willing to admit that beauty stuns, arrests, rips us out of our complacency, and lures us to distraction, perhaps even, if the beauty is truly magnificent, to bondage. And it does so completely without any other benefit. Helen's beauty eclipsed Troy, Cleopatra's beauty unseated a triumvir and laid waste the Nile, Mrs. Simpson brought down a British king, and Jodi Foster's beauty drove Hinckley to shoot an American president. The beauty of Alcibiades overweened the noblest thinker of them all, and Socrates lost his life not only for truth, but for beauty as well.

Beauty, then, like pleasure, guilt, and fate, is ultimate. Or rather, it is unlike the other three, though it is still ultimate. It is perhaps the most mysterious of the four, for it enslaves those who are most free, makes fools of the wisest, disarms the mightiest, brings down the loftiest, and elevates the lowest. But since it does these things without assistance, since beauty asks for no further reason, it too belongs as one of the four phenomena which we confront as ultimate. It can no more be explained than disregarded; yet it seems to make all things understandable. Though it is ultimate, it also bewilders.

These four phenomena show us what it means to confront either that which is inexplicable, like fate, or at least that which cannot be explained in terms beyond what is confronted, like guilt. In either case they show us what is meant by 'ultimate', at least in the sense that is being used in the present context. If they did nothing else, these four phenomena would be valuable in the attempt to understand truth as ultimate. But they are not merely four possible phenomena chosen among many. In anticipation of the argument which follows, it is possible to suggest now what later will be shown, that to take pleasure, to accept fate, to acknowledge guilt, and to submit to beauty are the four primordial ways in which our existence reveals what it means to confront truth. If this anticipatory suggestion is sound, it means that these four are not merely *examples* of what it means to confront truth, they are rather the fundamental existential ways that truth, as ultimate, is available to us.

At this juncture, of course, such a suggestion must await the considerable analysis necessary to make it intelligible. What must be done is to analyze these four existential phenomena to see whether they can be understood as providing access to truth *as a way of existing*. The above sketch of these four modalities is insufficient, for what is needed is an understanding of these phenomena as fundamental—that is, nonreducible—ways of being in truth. This fourfold list is therefore exclusive and central. It may seem arbitrary. Why, for example, is goodness not on the list, or logical certitude? But such questions, though entirely legitimate, must await the major interpretive task of the following section. Briefly the argument thus far can be summarized as follows: (1) truth, whether in the ordinary sense of true answers assumed by knowledge, or in the extraordinary sense of a terminal essence, means that which is ultimate; but (2) we seek to understand what it *means* to confront what is ultimate, and (3) the four fundamental ways in which we seem to be able to do this are pleasure, guilt, beauty, and fate. (4) We are therefore justified in characterizing these four existential phenomena as the faces of truth.

If the analysis is sufficient to support this claim, it would mean that we are capable of inquiring into truth only *because* we can take pleasure, be guilty and fated, and submit to beauty. It is only because we can do these four things that (1) truth can *matter at all,* and (2) we are *able* to inquire philosophically. Thus the analysis of the four faces of truth becomes of preeminent concern.

PART THREE
THE INQUIRER

7

The Faces of Truth: Pleasure and Fate

Pleasure

Few notions are as challenging to the philosopher as an analysis of pleasure. For pleasure is, by definition, that which all enjoy, and thus the entire population of the globe is critic, for whom no description can possibly be adequate. Furthermore, previous treatments have usually concerned the role pleasure plays — or does not play — in ethical discussions. Readers want to know whether pleasure is the same as goodness, or if not, why one should surrender so dear and intimate a motive to anything else. But the present inquiry is completely unconcerned with the morality or goodness of pleasure; rather it is concerned solely with the role, if any, that pleasure plays with regard to truth, and such a role apparently has no traditional support at all.

The task may be eased somewhat by the realization that 'pleasure' must be contrasted with 'gratification'. To gratify is to satisfy a hunger, a want, or a desire. Hence it is primarily a negative notion, understandable solely in terms of a dissatisfaction with a precedent state. The pain of hunger is relieved by the gratification we take in eating, the burning of lust is satisfied by the gratification we take in carnal release. Both animals and humans have gratification.

But in the strict, philosophical sense, pleasure means that satisfaction taken only by self-conscious beings solely for its own sake and not because of a prior prompting of need. To eat to assuage hunger is to gratify; to dine to please the palate is pleasure. Animals, it seems, do not take pleasure, they seek gratification. We can, and often do, mix the two, and whether there ever can be pure pleasure or pure gratification is an unimportant, contingent matter.

If on the one hand we must distinguish it from gratification, pleasure must also be separated from happiness, which is a much more complex and possibly even moral notion. Pleasure is far more immediate and existentially original than happiness, for I can ask whether I am *really* happy but not whether I am *really* having pleasure. The hedonist is indeed on far sounder ground existentially than the utilitarian, for pleasure is ultimate, and happiness quite obviously is not, though it is surely far more valuable and lasting. Certainly pleasure cannot be equated with goodness, even though in a colloquial sense we often say "that feels good" when what we really mean is that it pleases.

It may at first seem that pleasure is an entirely physical notion, requiring the existence of a body. But even if the mind/body distinction were not so dubious, there are those who speak of the pleasure of the mind; and since one must be conscious in order to have pleasure it seems ridiculous to limit this phenomenon to one side of an already questionable metaphysical dualism. Besides, the inquiry is not into the causes or conditions of pleasure, nor into the metaphysical faculties, but rather into what pleasure *means.*

How can one go about raising such an intimate and immediate question? Pleasure pleases. Why do we need to know anything beyond that? Indeed, if the entire question depends upon the *ultimacy* of pleasure, then surely any account beyond the analytic one, pleasure pleases, would be misleading, explaining what is simple by the artificial complexity of abstraction. Nevertheless, the difficulty of analysis must be overcome. It may be possible to begin by recognizing that the purposive account of gratification cannot illuminate the present inquiry. We recognize that were we not impelled to eat by the provocation of hunger we would die, and if the carnal urges were not present the species would disappear, and so the natural explanation of pleasure lies in its purposive structure which accounts for the continuation of the species. But this again confuses pleasure with gratification. Suppose I eat, not because I am hungry, but simply because it tastes good. In such a case I eat because it brings pleasure, not because it stops my hunger. The pleasure taken in taste must therefore be understood nonpurposively. But what does this tell us about who we are? What kind of being am I that takes pleasure for no reason other than that it pleases? To sip a rare wine that blossoms unexpectedly with untaxed generosity on the tongue; to thrill to the glory of the rapid descent down the powdery ski slope, a friend to the trees; to nestle snugly before a crackling fire as the wind shrieks harmlessly beyond the stout cabin walls; to smell seductive bestowals from lilacs and lilies of the valley on a newborn spring day — these are not to fulfill a purpose but to be fulfilled. Pleasure, especially when exquisite, positively rejects the grim purposiveness of nature. Indeed we do not even want to be told *why* we enjoy these things, lest in learning of their reason we lose sight of their very grace. To this extent, pleasure is *unnatural,* that is, delight is taken entirely because it satisfies no prior need or want.

But this in itself is an extraordinary realization. What does it mean to be free from purely naturalistic explanations? The question itself almost stuns the mind. Is there some divine being who bestows these useless but wonderful delights simply because he is fond of us? Such an argument cannot be sustained, of course; though if there ever were a meaningful argument for God's existence it would be this one, that if pleasure cannot be explained purposively it must be explained by an appeal to our gratitude for undeserved delights, and this gratitude must have as its object a loving donor who is called God. It is its status as undeserved that makes pleasure so compelling.

It is common enough to appeal to the pleasure principle as an entirely natural explanation, as if pleasure were a kind of gravity explaining the fall of rocks. But upon analysis it seems that nothing is less natural than pleasure, for nature demands causes and responses to need. Nature has no room for gratuity, but the real pleasure of pleasure is that it is entirely gratuitous. There is nothing that says I *ought* or *should* enjoy the smell of a rose, and there is no purpose in it either. Something should be said for the sheer wonder of pleasure. Severed entirely from the grim mechanism of nature, the strictures of morality, and the heavy insistence on purpose, pleasure delights and elevates, excites and soothes, and when honored, even prods the mind to wonder. A life without pleasure is so unspeakable it darkens all thought. When the question is raised as to the meaning of pleasure, the cheerful difficulty consists in trying to understand why it should be questioned at all. Only the most mistrustful find in pleasure deviation from the good. Because of pleasure we can reward the deserving, manifest our love, celebrate what should be honored, comfort the distressed, and simply enjoy to the fullest the fleeting tenure of our lives.

Pleasure, however, is often the culprit in distracting us from our duty. This must be admitted, but to recognize it further enhances our respect for the power of pleasure. For it cannot be an engine of small moment that would derail our journey down the path of righteousness. Even in its ability to tempt us from being good the allure of pleasure testifies to its importance and significance. Besides, it is not usually pleasure itself that leads us astray, but pleasure in excess or pleasure perverted or pleasure conjoined with other vices.

What, then, does it mean to be pleased, or to be able to take pleasure at all? It is to be able to receive approvingly what need not be. It is to assent or to affirm our own private capacity to feel at all. Indeed, to take pleasure is *to feel*, that is, to be the receptor of impressions, beyond the range of being a cause or an effect. Precisely because pleasure, unlike gratification, which is recognized as purposive, is *free* from such dependence, it therefore serves as the most fundamental way in which our existence is shown to matter. To take pleasure is to *affirm* the uninevitability of our response to what affects us.

But pleasure, though it is ubiquitous, nevertheless reveals its truest nature in its rarer instances. To taste an exquisite sauce is to discover what it means to taste at all. To hear a glorious symphony is to discover what it means to hear at all. Sexual pleasure may be the most intense, but it is so often dominated by gratification of the *need* to satisfy our venereal urgency that it may not always provide the best resource for understanding; furthermore, it is often enough coupled with the loftier passion of love, so that what *pleases* in sex may be overshadowed by gratification and love. Nevertheless the true pleasure taken in sex reveals what it means to be *as* a male or female. Carnal pleasure reveals to a male what it means to be masculine and to a female what it means to be feminine. These are not items of individual discovery in the school of lust. The pleasures of sex reveal to men the meaning of their masculinity; perhaps such pleasures even *are* the meaning of masculinity. Thus, pleasure becomes a source, and in some cases *the* source, of learning what it means to exist in these absolutely fundamental ways — tasting (not 'eating'), hearing, seeing, being male or female, having senses, being able to feel at all. In revealing what it means to exist on such fundamental levels, pleasure provides us with a terminus which encloses the interrogation.

And it is in this phase of the argument that the distinction between gratification and pleasure reveals itself in its full import. Gratification terminates the desire; pleasure encloses the existential wonder. We *learn* in pleasure (and not "from" pleasure, which would suggest a secondary role) *as it pleases.* What we learn is what it means to hear, to feel, to be sexual, to taste; and we *learn* in pleasure precisely because pleasure is *other* than gratification, which does not teach us anything but releases us from the pain of wanting or deserving.

But to say that pleasure *reveals* what it means to taste or to be male or female is to understand pleasure as a source of *truth*. How can a mere feeling provide information? Of course, pleasure is not a mere feeling, it is that which makes feeling intelligible by allowing for affirmation and negation. Pleasure is not the *what* but the *how* of feeling, and because in pleasure one affirms one's capacity to feel, and in pain and suffering one rejects or denies this capacity, feeling itself is capable of being thought.

These reflections show the philosophical superiority of raising fundamental questions existentially rather than metaphysically. A metaphysical dualist, such as Descartes, would insist that the fundamental question is always "What kind of thing exists?" and so would couch the present discussion in terms of the entity 'body' which is defined as taking up space. This entity, body, which *is* only insofar as it is in space, can receive stimuli from external sources, some of which cause positive reactions *within* the body, and this is called pleasure. But the existential inquiry avoids the metaphysical assertion and asks directly about what it means to feel. Feeling can be understood by appealing to two pairs of existential opposites: to be in pain and to be gratified is what it *means* to 'have a body'; to suffer and to take pleasure is what it *means* to have 'a mind in a body'—but the metaphysical language now has a derived or secondary status. Feeling explains the 'body', not the other way around; feeling thoughtfully explains the 'mind'. Both body and mind are therefore made intelligible by reference to the ontologically prior notions of *being* satisfied or dissatisfied.

Taking up space, being extended, may well be a necessary and perhaps even sufficient condition for an external object, but these conditions cannot explain our own body or our own mind, for the latter are not objects *of* our cognition but faculties *by which* we have cognition. Enduring suffering or taking pleasure reveals what it means to feel, and if we argue that 'feeling' requires a body as receptor and a mind to account for the awareness, such inferences may be helpful, but the ensuing metaphysical description of these two entities, body and mind, simply cannot be more fundamental than the modalities of existence which explain them. At best, body and mind become convenient assumptions which may make identificatory and classificatory enterprises easier. Therefore, the existential distinction between pain and gratification on the one hand and suffering and pleasure on the other are superior to the metaphysical distinction between body and mind, because the latter can only be *objects* of our cognition but the former are *ways by which* we cognize at all. And as such, pleasure and suffering are confrontations of truth.

If we submit as two candidates of how we make sense of body (1) the feelings of pleasure and pain and (2) taking up space, we recognize that they represent two entirely different approaches: the latter may explain the body as one among many possible objects, but the former explains what it means to be a body. If pleasure is to confront the truth, it must be understood in that existential sense.

It may be thought that if pleasure confronts the truth as ultimate, then the opposite would not confront truth. But this is not the case. Existentially, the "opposite" of pleasure is not pain but suffering; and suffering is the negative pole of this confrontation. The *contradictory* of pleasure is not pain or suffering, but anesthesia — not feeling at all. But, unlike pleasure, suffering does not confront the ultimate, for it demands to be explained, whereas we have just seen that pleasure terminates the demand. And so we must now examine the counterprinciple of pleasure. What does suffering mean?

Suffering

How do we think about suffering? Some thinkers insist on raising this question in terms of theodicy: suffering is evil, evil is inconsistent with a good and powerful divinity, but since suffering is real it follows that God is not. What seems incredible about this argument is not that it proves the impossibility of God — for it does not do that — but rather that it is intended in some way to tell us about suffering. Suffering is submitted as 'that which is inconsistent with a rational and good universe.' Suffering, therefore, does not make sense. Apparently it is easier for an atheist to accept a senseless universe than it is for a theist, though why this should be so is never explained. Does the problem cease merely because one abandons belief in God? If suffering is evil it will *still be* evil even if God does *not* exist, and why nature should be evil is just as unintelligible as why God should allow it. The question is, how must we think of suffering? Whether suffering is evil must await the analysis of this prior question.

There are, of course, instances in which suffering is *not* evil; indeed there are cases in which suffering actually can be affirmed as something we are glad can occur. The first of these is justice. If justice is understood properly as the reward of the good and the punishment of the wicked, then *if* someone has done something bad, we are glad that he can suffer, because if he could not, we could not achieve justice. Thus, if justice is to matter, the wrongdoer must be able to suffer — and we must affirm this even and especially if that wrongdoer is ourself. Thus the very intelligibility of justice demands that suffering be affirmed.

A far more fascinating justification of suffering is found in sacrifice. To sacrifice is to endure suffering as a form of bestowal upon one whom we love or honor. To sacrifice is to "give of oneself" to the extent that this "giving" is a gift and not a reward, and that the giving costs us what is dear and precious. It would be impossible to sacrifice in a world in which there were no suffering. But lovers not only are willing to sacrifice, they *want* to sacrifice, and to that extent suffering is precious because it allows for loving.

Nevertheless, suffering is unlike its opposite, pleasure, in that it does not provide us with a terminus to a series of whys. Yet, like pleasure, suffering cannot be understood solely in terms of natural events — though pain can be explained that way. Pain has a purpose: the burning on my hand hurts and causes me to pull it away from the hot stove. I understand this as a protective device in nature, and although I do not like the pain, the fact that my body has functioned properly in warning me at least makes it intelligible. Suffering, however, seems an assault on my conscious existence and on my meaning. How can I think about suffering?

It may be beneficial to consider what is often called "mental anguish," to ensure that the purely "painful" elements do not distract from the analysis. A young man suffers because of the death of his bride of only eight months. His grief is terrible because he loved her passionately; and so he suffers. Yet, if he were asked: do you wish to be relieved of your grief? he might hesitate. If it were possible for a laser to burn out of his brain precisely those cells which retained his memory of her, he might well refuse to submit to this therapy. The enormity of his grief, he may realize, simply is due to the enormity of his love. Had he not loved so much then, he would not grieve so much now. He may wish he could go back in time, or that she had not died, but even in his extremity he realizes the futility of such thinking. Thus, although he may bitterly resent his need to suffer and grieve, he would not opt *not* to grieve at her death, for that would mean her death did not matter. Thus some kinds of suffering, as in grief, cannot be forsworn without the forfeiture of something so precious that the suffering demands acceptance.

In all of these cases, however, the suffering is endured for the sake of something else. The husband accepts the suffering caused by his grief because grieving is part of what it means to love at all. In fact, "I love you" may well entail "I would grieve at your absence." Or, we say we can affirm our suffering because if we could not sacrifice we could not love, so once again love, which is usually seen as a positive phenomenon, justifies suffering. In the case of justice we recognize that if we could not suffer we could not punish, and without punishment there would be no justice, so justice explains suffering. Thus, suffering, unlike its existential opposite, pleasure, is not self-justifying or ultimate, but it retains its existential significance.

Nevertheless, it is pleasure and not its opposite, suffering, which provides us with a confrontation of truth as ultimate. In order to discover what is ultimate through suffering we must focus solely on suffering which is not endured for the sake of anything else, which is the second face of truth.

Fate

When the meaning of fate is approached by way of the more spectacular examples, such as the woman struck by paralysis, the danger lies in the fear and loathing that these examples provoke. Fate is seen as cruel and indifferent and curiously selective, as if only the very few were singled out to bear the terrible burdens of fortune, examples to the rest of us warning what could happen. But of course this is absurd. All of us are fated, and at times the sheer improbability of chance adventures that seriously or trivially alter our lives prompts us to wonder about who we are. Had I not remained longer than usual in the office, I would not have met this person, who changed my life. Had the train not been late I would have been able to make this opportunity which would have radically improved my fortune. From chance encounters, to pieces of luck, to lottery tickets, to the military draft, to the color of our eyes and the seat on the plane, we are thrown into situations and events quite beyond our control or even our comprehension. It makes no difference whether we believe in a divine providence or in the sheer randomness of nature, the point is, such important influences in our lives are totally beyond our understanding or control, and it is precisely because such enormously important circumstances cannot be understood in the ordinary way that we are forced to wonder: how do we think about fate at all? Is it better simply to recognize the futility of such a question, and hence develop psychological attitudes to help us avoid considering it altogether, or is it more honest to confront the unrooted truth or our fate and seek to find a way to think about it?

But when it comes to the question of how we think about fate, bewilderment seems inescapable. It is easy enough to recognize, whether we call it luck or chance or fortune or the general randomness of things; but when we try to think about it there seem to be no guides or hints. Perhaps, then, we simply do not *think* about fate at all. To appeal to it is nothing more than to admit it is beyond the range of comprehension altogether.

Yet, human culture is not quite so impoverished. Fate, luck, and chance, as well as all the other imponderables of our species, attract our finest minds, if for no other reason than that they challenge the limits of our self-esteem. There is an art form singularly well suited to reveal what it means to be fated. From the terrifying magnificence of Aeschylus, down through Shakespeare, to O'Neill and Williams, the tragedians have actually celebrated fate, and in so doing have made available for us a method for confronting it. If nothing else, tragedy reminds us of fate. But since in reminding us of it these gifted titans of human thought also illuminate it, the role fate plays in the tragic dramas may well be the single best resource available to save us from mere dismissal of so important a notion. If tragedy's remarkable treatment of fate is but diligently and carefully analyzed, perhaps this elusive but paramount notion will be rendered open to inquiry.

We are told in the opening chorus that the exquisite love between the young Montague and the even younger Capulet is star-crossed; and as early as the first act Romeo himself recognizes he is "fortune's fool." Shakespeare takes great pains to assure his audience that the most important elements in his tale of woe turn on the most freakish of accidents. Friar Laurence's devilish plan should have worked; there was no likely reason why his envoy to Mantua should not have reached Romeo in time. Had Juliet awakened from her enchanted sleep only a few minutes earlier, the lovers could have escaped and maybe resolved the ancient enmity of the two houses with their marriage. The play is rife with slender ifs and onlys. It almost seems the playwright dangles success before us only to tantalize us by the unlikely failures.

And yet, the impact of the play is not one of frustration with barely missed opportunities. We do not leave the theater cursing the bad luck that robs the young lovers over and over again during the course of the play. Rather, as the story unfolds there is a curious logic of inevitability which seems to doom their love from the very opening lines. Watching the play we sense that their loving as well as their dying is inevitable. They are, we sense, fated to die. But *this* use of the term is entirely antithetical to the earlier sense which implies sheer accident, random occurrences, and wanton chance. How can a story which specifically spells out the *arbitrariness* of the grim events nevertheless entail the irresistible conviction that their suffering *had* to happen?

There can be no mistake about it. It is sheer fortuity that brings Romeo to the Capulets' party, sheer chance that he and Juliet should meet, entirely unlikely they should love, almost incomprehensible they should fail, wildly improbable they should die as they do. But neither can it be denied that, as the play unfolds, they *must* love, they *must* find themselves locked in a cruel dilemma, and they *must* take their lives, almost as certainly as winter trails the autumn. How are we to make sense of this?

We are, of course, told in the opening chorus that they die. Perhaps we feel the inevitability of the tragic end merely because the poet from Stratford is an enchanter; he has merely *written* it so that it *seems* inevitable. But of course he has. It is, after all, a work of art, not a historical account. But why should that *be* the nature of his genius? Granted it is a fictional tale, why should the story succeed when wrought with this logic of inevitability? The protest that we cannot learn from it because it is art defies all reason. Perhaps we learn from it only *because* it is art.

The inevitability of fate, which seems an almost universally accepted perception of tragedies, is revealed only in the telling of a story, not in the analysis of isolated events. Isolated events are intelligible solely by reference to causal explanations, or in the case of human acts, possibly purposive explanation. But events as part of a story, fact or fictive, are intelligible by the inner necessity of the unfolding theme. To understand the character is to understand his story, to understand who he is is to understand what must happen to him. But the *knowledge* of such inevitability is simply not available to anyone prior to the events, and so it would seem that stories, even if they are *true,* do not *explain;* rather they simply entertain the listener by appealing to forces which do not exist in the world, like magic, miracle, the efficacy of prayer, or fate.

Yet, stories *do* seem to explain, and the incomprehensibility of wanton chance is no less offensive to reason than the illuminative power of stories. So powerful is the seeming inevitability found in stories, particularly tragic ones, that Heraclitus was led to assert that our character *is* our fate. The fact that knowledge of one's character should therefore reveal one's fate disturbs not at all, since neither fate *nor* character is ever available to us to test in this way. Certainly, however, if fate is a face of truth, it seems to be reflected in the tragic mirror.

There thus seem to be two possible ways of thinking about fate. In the first case, fate is simply what happens, and there is no intelligibility or reasoning to explain it. The word 'fate' in this sense is merely a confession of fundamental ignorance or even fundamental irrationality. In the second case, fate is that which would make the events inevitable if the story were but known, and when the story *is* known the specter of fate looms as a kind of aesthetic principle which provides intelligibility of a sort, but not an explanation in the sense that we can *use* it to our advantage. Fateful *inevitability,* of the sort that seems present in tragic art, is not the same as *predictability.* To have knowledge of what conditions bring about snow is to be able to predict snow, but to see that Lear's fate, given his character and the circumstances of the story, is inevitable is to recognize that the story could not have developed any other way, which is *not* to say one would *know* the outcome of the story before it is told. The absence of this prestory knowledge relieves tragic inevitability of the onus of predictability. Perhaps, therefore, this is precisely what we *mean* by fate: not that it can ever be predicted, but that its unfolding makes us aware of its intelligibility. What makes this postfactual unfolding intelligible just is its ability to reinterpret the random events as a storied series of events. Stories are thinkable but not predictable.

The real protest, therefore, is not that fate is irrational—which it would be if it were merely a random event—but that it is not knowable in advance and hence not controllable. It remains open to us as a source of meaning only because it can tell a story; but it is not open to us as predictable behavior. What this tells us about ourselves is ultimate, however, and in this sense fate remains a face of truth.

'To explain', therefore, reveals itself as having two distinct meanings: to make knowable, and hence controllable, as when a scientist explains to his students which chemicals react and how they react; and to show how something fits into a broader picture, as when a historian shows his student how the ills of the industrial revolution provide an ongoing story in which the subsequent social upheavals make entirely good sense. The laws of history cannot particularize or even predict specific events, as the laws of chemistry can, but after the events occur they can be rendered 'thinkable' by means of a story, and hence are explainable. Fate is not a *cause* or a *purpose,* but it still is thinkable.

Fate remains a confrontation with that which cannot be explained in any other way. It is a part of the very *meaning* of fate that it is incomprehensible, but this curiously does not mean that all who accept fate are irrational. Whatever is experienced is contingent, and insofar as it is contingent it is not necessary; and not being necessary it is not a product of pure reason. But no one would say that what is contingent is irrational. It might be said to be nonrational, meaning it is not known necessarily; but the term 'irrational' is usually reserved for that which directly contradicts itself, like an odd number wholly divisible by two, or a married bachelor. Fate is troubling and perhaps even nonrational, but it is certainly not irrational.

Tragedy is not merely about fate, however; it is also about undeserved suffering, which, like fate, seems to confound our ordinary ways of thinking. Precisely because Antigone does not deserve her misfortune we are challenged to seek other resources which allow us to come to grips with the dramatic impact. It is not enough to say simply that it is Antigone's fate to be treated unfairly. If that were enough, fate would become a dustbin into which the mind could cheerfully toss all of its unsolvable trash, dismissing it from the cleaned house of reason. Tragic plays are not junkyards or cesspools; we must ask what allows theater owners to take our money in exchange for showing us these representations of such irrational things as fate and undeserved suffering.

By focusing on the unsuccess of noble beings, tragedy requires us to isolate the greatness of the characters from the wretchedness of their lives. Who they are becomes greater than what they do and what happens to them. The technique of the tragic dramatist is to place his hero in such unwholesome adventure that we *cannot* approve of what happens to him. But at the same time the dramatist makes the protagonist so noble in character, so worthy of our attention and admiration, that we are compelled to affirm his existence in spite of his misery. By sequestering the worth of his existence from the success of his endeavors we achieve a remarkable elevation of mind, and an aesthetic reaction so curiously satisfying that we are led to rank the tragic art as among the most sublime.

All moral interpretations of tragedy, therefore, including Aristotle's, are deeply misleading, and should be rejected as fraudulent deceptions. The overriding passion one feels at the conclusion of *King Lear* or *Antigone* is *not* satisfaction that justice has been achieved or the result of a recognition that the heroes somehow deserve their agony because of some "tragic flaw" in their makeup. Rather it is precisely the opposite: realizing that there is *no* moral justification, we reach beyond the ethical limits and seek to find alternative ground for our ennobled response. Since all ethical and moral elements have been deliberately removed, we are left with the worth of the characters themselves. Their existential worth stands naked and unadorned by happiness and even justice. The very fact that the audience can find such enormous approval for *who* they are, in spite of the terrible wretchedness of what has befallen them, represents the supreme achievement of the dramatist's art. The worth of Antigone matters most when the events which happen to Antigone make us recoil in horror. This is the triumph of who one is over happiness and unhappiness, and that discovery is of a truth so magnificent in its meaning that it deserves celebration, a Dionysian celebration.

The triumph of existential worth over happiness is obviously intimately connected with the inevitability of fate. Just as our ordinary thinking about what is important supports the utilitarian doctrine that happiness is the *summum bonum*, so our ordinary thinking about what is intelligible supports the world of predictability. The triumph *over* happiness in tragedy and the triumph over predictability in the celebration of fate can only be seen as offensive and dangerous to these ordinary ways of thinking. But the inevitability of fate and the triumph of character over fortune are irresistible challenges. We avoid them at the peril of untruth; for to deny the truth which tragedy reveals can only be the grossest form of self-deception.

The inevitability of fate provides a kind of "logic" in which the triumph over undeserved suffering can be thought. In the telling of the story the noble character seems destined to endure his agonies; this "destiny" becomes intelligible as the lawlikeness of the unfolding story makes its aesthetic appeal. The very nature of a story renders the notion of fate intelligible, though not predictable or controllable. And of course it is precisely because fate is neither predictable nor controllable, and yet at the same time *is thinkable* by the logic of the unfolding story, that it *confronts* us as an ultimate face of truth.

But even as we accept this autonomy of fate from utilitarian reasoning, the question remains: is it not *better* and hence more rational to have a *controlled* life than a fated one?

An ancient thinker once submitted this pattern of reasoning. Of three lives, the life of pleasure, that of honor, and that of reflection, the first two are dependent on elements outside of us. Pleasure depends on fortune, and honor depends on the fickle judgment of other men. But reflection or philosophical contemplation of truth, being independent, is superior. It is revealing to focus not on whether this argument is convincing, but on the presupposition that it is better to control one's life than to have it controlled. Intuitively this seems quite sound, for if the good life depends solely on our commitment to truth the chances of failure seem less. But Aristotle, who offers this argument in the *Nicomachean Ethics,* is not convinced that the success rate is important; rather he takes it as intuitively obvious that simply because the life of reflection is independent it is a better life. The sheer difficulty of searching after the truth may lower the success rate below that of the lives of pleasure or honor, but since it is still autonomous the reflective life is judged superior.

Another ancient thinker found his own good fortune worthy of reflection and gratitude. He accepted his happiness as a bestowal, and argued that the acknowledgment of his fortune as a bestowal was the wisest and most glorious response possible. When the cast of his fate changed darkly, and miseries and misfortunes began to follow in an almost comical reversal of his earlier delights, he continued to accept his bestowals graciously. His friends urged him to curse his fate and to turn his back on these bestowals, but he refused. He had accepted his earlier good fortune not merely because it was good but because it was his fortune. Whatever was bestowed was his, and he considered it better to embrace bestowal regardless of whether the bestowal were fair or foul. If we put Aristotle next to Job before our minds, what do we see? For the Greek thinker, it is clear that autonomy and control is simply more rational. This epitomizes ordinary thinking; but since it is done by a supreme master, it is ordinary thinking at its very best. Aristotle is not so foolish as to argue that the man of reflection will never suffer pain or be abandoned by the fellowship of men. He simply argues that fortune and honor are not as constant, and hence not as worthy, as that which is controlled. And we must agree that his argument is sound.

Job on the other hand is also a wise man. His insights are also compelling, but they fly in the face of ordinary thought. The difference between Job and Aristotle is not that between the believer and the rational inquirer, nor is it the difference between faith and reason. For Job the question is: what does it mean to be able to be bestowed *at all?* For his remarkable position is *not* a naive trust that God will always do that which is in the long run better for us. This argument, often heard from theological apologists, simply amounts to a denial that there is any evil at all; it is merely our ignorance that keeps us from seeing the hidden benefits in apparent misfortune. Job's wisdom is not that shallow; for when his miseries attack him he does *not* accept them as benefits in disguise, but as miseries. What is so extraordinary about the wisdom of Job is that he recognizes what it means to be the kind of being to whom anything is given at all.

An analysis of the presuppositions behind the meaning of various forms of possession may reveal the significance of this kind of thinking. I may look at my own hand and ask: what must be presupposed in order to make sense of my having this hand? If I am alert enough to the rules of genetic inheritance it may be that the only presupposition I need to make is nature itself. Indeed, the care given to me by my mother may possibly be due solely to the inherited instincts of the species, and hence even my basic animal nurture assumes only the natural laws which govern such phenomena. Suppose, however, I consider my wage, earned by my labor and agreed upon by contact. In order to make sense of the possessions which I own by dint of this labor, it is not enough merely to presuppose the laws of nature. I must also presuppose the laws of society, governed by the principles of justice. In other words, the goods which I possess because I purchased them with money I have earned *make sense* only because I can presuppose the validity of justice and the historical founding of a government that protects these fundamental rights. Both *nature,* which accounts for my physical possessions like hands and feet, as well as the nurture provided by my parents due to their inherited instincts, and *justice,* which accounts for my employer giving me a decent wage for my labors, are within the realm of intelligibility shared by Aristotle and Job alike.

Suppose, however, that I am given a gift, not a wage or a natural inheritance. What must I assume now? As long as a gift is truly distinct from what is earned or inherited by nature, I must assume some other kind of reason for the bestowal. Who am I to receive unearned gifts? At the very least I must assume that who I am, as opposed to what I do and hence deserve, somehow merits or explains this bestowal. Thus, *if* there are genuine gifts *at all,* then neither nature nor justice can account for them. Rather I must assume that *who* I am, as opposed to *what* I am or what I have *done,* matters in some way. We give gifts to those who belong to us, either by the bond of affection or by the bonds of sharing a common realm, like a family. The very point of a gift is that it is not necessary. A bestowal, therefore, if it is to be *thought,* requires the presupposition of belonging or affection. Just as a parent bestows a gift on a child simply because the child is *his,* and not because the child has earned it or needs it to function in health and security, so Job recognizes that to accept bestowals is to presuppose that he matters in this special way. It is, of course, neither just nor unjust to receive bestowals, for gifts are not made sense of by an appeal to what is earned. Since it cannot be *just* to receive a gift, neither can it be *unjust* to receive an unfortunate bestowal.

One's proper response to gifts is gratitude; and Job was grateful for his good fortune. But Job was not grateful for his miseries, for that would be perverse. His friends make the following appeal: if it makes sense to be grateful when the bestowals are fair, does it not also make sense to curse when the bestowals are foul? But to curse is to reject bestowals altogether; rather Job realizes that there is a special kind of recognition which retains respect for the institution of bestowing but which is not the same as gratitude, and this is endurance. For Job is not so unnatural as to be glad that he suffers; rather he recognizes the truth that if gratitude is a meaningful response, ingratitude is a meaningless response. To accept his fate as a bestowal is therefore a kind of wisdom. But wisdom is the confrontation of truth, not advantage.

And with this step we see that Aristotle and Job are much more akin than they are alien, for both see the ultimate worth in truth. The wisdom of these two ancient titans is awesome, and both are essential. But in seeking to confront fate, Job has approached truth more surely than Aristotle. It is, of course, impossible to grasp Job's wisdom without realizing his trust in a bestowing God; but it is possible to isolate the meaning of fate without making any metaphysical presupposition. Fate is here disclosed as a kind of bestowal, and this means that we must think about it the same way we think about gifts, as indications that who we are matters. From reflection on the nature of tragedy we learn that fate is an inevitability without predictability unfolded in a story. If we combine these two discoveries we can now provisionally suggest that fate is the confrontation of truth as inevitable bestowal. As ultimate, it is a way we exist *in truth*. This means it cannot be explained by any reference to whys or causes, but it is thinkable in the way stories link otherwise unconnected events together by the power of narrative. Not all stories make the events inevitable, however; only tragedy does this, and it does so by isolating the worth of the hero's existence from his happiness or the justice of his suffering. Both the tragic emphasis upon character and the isolation of who we are in the phenomenon of bestowal reveal the existential importance of fate. Fate, like pleasure, is a confrontation of ultimacy, and hence must be seen as a face of truth.

Freedom

If by fate we mean that aspect of our existence over which we have no control, then there must be a counteraspect over which we do have control. Freedom, however, cannot be fundamentally understood in terms of having choices, for most choices that I have are mine to make only because I am fortunate enough to have them, and that means they are choices because I am fated. If I freely choose to deceive my friend I must first be fortunate enough to have friends and even more fortunate enough to be able to do things about it. Nevertheless, freedom is not a trivial notion. How must we think about it? Although Aristotle does not use the term freedom, it is obvious that his presupposition that a life in control is superior to a life out of control implies that autonomy matters. Furthermore, this autonomy is achieved only by a life of thought. The best of all possible ways to live, therefore, is one in which thinking frees us from arbitrariness—which it can indeed do up to a point, though not even thinking can free us from fate. Thinking achieves autonomy not by providing us with options or choices, but by providing us with a nonarbitrary source of our worth: truth. The other possible candidates which Aristotle offers, pleasure and honor, are rejected solely on the grounds that they are arbitrary and random, perhaps even wanton. Why does this constancy provide autonomy? Why am I not just as autonomous, and hence free, if I follow the fickle adulations of men in the life of honor, or the fleeting delights offered by pleasure? Is it not better to have fleeting pleasures than constant dreariness? Where is it guaranteed that truth will always be worthy of our dedication? Surely it is not the *mere* constancy which makes it precious; there is constancy in death and nothingness as well.

But there is a grinding consistency to the argument that is relentless. What frees Job from being a slave either to his happiness or to his misery is how he *thinks* about it. What frees Aristotle from the inconstancy of pleasure and honor is his ranking of *thought* above these other boons. But what is it that makes thinking *possible?* The answer to this is not the Enlightenment's answer. What makes thinking possible is not the mind, or reason, or judgment, or even the ability to solve problems. What makes thinking possible is truth. For if truth were not a meaningful notion which, on its own, mattered, I could not think. To be able to think is the fundamental meaning of being free. To be autonomous is to think, and thinking is possible only because truth matters. Truth therefore is the ground of freedom.

However, it is pleasure and fate which confront truth, not their opposites, suffering and freedom. In this analysis of truth as ultimate, fate is more significant than freedom. There can be no doubt that we, as human beings, are both fated and free, and so it might seem that both fate and freedom equally confront truth. But freedom is not self-explanatory or ultimate as fate is, precisely because freedom can be explained in a way that fate cannot. There is, of course, a further notion involved when we think of freedom, and that is the irreducible and inescapable responsibility which burdens us as inevitably as fate. But this must be approached not through the abstract notion of freedom, but in the existential immediacy of guilt.

8
The Faces of Truth: Guilt and Beauty

Guilt

Fingers point. Eyes accuse. The guilty acknowledge their guilt. Truth irresistibly and irrevocably burdens with negation. There is no more powerful realization of denial in the entire arsenal of human consciousness. To be a self at all is to be able to be guilty.

The argument is as clear as any in the philosophical repertoire. If I am incapable of guilt; if, that is, I am not responsible for what I do; if the actions which I perform are in fact caused by antecedent conditions, or if they are determined by complex laws of nature, then there is no "I" aside from my bodily referent, at all. For if my actions and the inherent responsibility of them are indeed due to factors and conditions which are explainable by nature, then *I* have no role in them. If the insult to my friend is the inevitable result of prior conditions, and if the kindness to my friend is likewise explainable by these antecedent factors, then any meaningful sense of an autonomous, worthwhile "I" is entirely forfeit. For if my wrongdoing is explained by such external factors, then the action is neither mine nor wrong. Not only is 'being wrong' an illusion, but so too is 'being me' an illusion. What could it possibly mean to say there is a 'self' if it cannot *do* anything? How can there be a "me" if all that happens occurs because of something else? The rock that causes a landslide has no "self" either. I can neither initiate action nor even think of myself as counting for anything in the vast intercourse of the human species. To deny guilt is to matter not at all. To be incapable of guilt is to disappear altogether from the lexicon of meaningful events.

I may, of course, protest that I am not guilty of a particular act; but this is to assume I could be guilty. To be innocent of a specific wrong is possible only if I am able to be guilty at all. It is almost incredible to read and listen to intelligent people speculate on the so-called problem of freedom or determinism. If all that I do is in fact determined by natural causes, then my belief in and assertion of determinism is itself determined—that is, I cannot help believing in determinism—and then truth itself ceases to be a meaningful notion. For I *must* believe *x* if I am determined to believe *x,* and hence whether *x* is really true is simply irrelevant.

To say that *I* exist is to imply that it matters that I exist; but unless I can be held responsible for what I do there is no way that I can matter. By *modus tollens,* then, if I cannot be guilty I simply cannot *be.* This physical body might exist, but it cannot consciously be "my" body, since what is "mine" depends on a meaningful notion of who I am. If all that I do is ultimately traced back to factors other than myself, a meaningful notion of who I am disappears.

Being guilty is thus an essential characteristic of meaningful self-consciousness. Perhaps it is even more than that. Guilt may well be the ultimacy of self-realization which makes possible being in truth at all. To be guilty is to be in truth.

Let us assume a man is accused of cruelty to a child. Let us further assume there is no question of the facts involved; the man himself admits he did the acts for which he is indicted. But he and his attorney argue that he was under compulsion to act in this way: he *had* to do it. The psychological circumstances of his own childhood and the environmental factors since then were such that he simply could not resist the inclination to abuse the child. This is to say, perhaps, that his own capacity to act responsibly was too weak or insufficiently developed to counter the external influences which led him to the act. This we can understand and pity, for it means that his own will—who he really is—does not matter as much as external forces. We pity this person, and demand that he no longer be allowed his liberty because he cannot control himself. He is not punished because he is, in an authentic sense, not guilty.

But now let us assume that a quite different argument is made. Now the assertion is made that, as a human being, he is fundamentally incapable ever of being the agent of a human act. This is not to indict him of insufficient moral strength, which may extenuate or even excuse. Rather, it is to say that *he* does not matter at all, that the psychological conditions and environmental factors totally exhaust all explanative forces that make up his existence. In the first case we might find him innocent by means of reduced capacity; but in the second we find him not even morally significant. That is, who *he* is simply does not matter; the *sole* determining factors are those which make up his environment — though we should perhaps not even say this; rather we should say the sole factors are those which make up *the* (not "his") environment, since quite seriously there is no "his." To what does the term "his" refer? Certainly not an agent. In this account "he" has simply disappeared.

Finally let us — if we can still say "we" and "us" — assume that this radical incapacity for being held responsible is a universal condition of all mankind. Such a situation, since it would be an event, could not not occur; it would have to be the case. We then would all vanish. But the assumption is retained because it is the only assumption consistent with the laws of nature, which require that every event have a cause. Such an assumption cannot be *true,* since it, too, is merely determined by nature. Not only do "we" cease, but so does all sense. We cannot think — or rather, since the pronoun is gratuitous, thinking cannot be.

This *reductio ad absurdum* reveals the fundamental necessity of guilt as a truth without which thinking could not occur. If an *argument* is given — which requires thought in order to *be* an argument — that guilt is an illusion, then both thinking and truth are illusions. However, the value of the *reductio* does not consist in showing that there must *be* guilt; rather it shows what it *means* to be guilty. To be guilty is to be a self, where 'self' merely means that who one is does indeed matter.

Let us now assume that the man indicted of cruelty to the child acknowledges his guilt. He still admits his childhood and environment were conducive to violence, and that psychological factors made it difficult for him to restrain himself. But he acknowledges a nonnecessary submission to these base impulses, and confesses that in yielding to them he did what he ought not to have done. The term 'ought' is a crucial and important moral notion, but for the child abuser it is rather the term 'not' which is dominant. For this 'not' is the fundamental meaning of his guilt. It is not the case that this 'not' is first discovered in some logical capacity to negate; rather in guilt the 'not' is acknowledged as meaningful, and only because it is meaningful can it then provide the purely formal capacity to negate. The 'not' of guilt is prior to logical negation, for in guilt one is meaningful because one acknowledges the lack, the failure, the negation built into one's very ability to affirm or deny at all.

The negation entailed in guilt is also a cessation of the causal series. In acknowledging guilt one cuts off any appeal to further explanations, and in so doing leaves oneself isolated and naked. There is no further psychological account, no description necessary of what it is like to feel guilty, for the separation from redemptive reasoning is as profound as one can get. Acknowledging guilt is not merely *explaining* what is the ground, it is *being* the ground. There is no further account, for guilt is the ultimate account. "I am guilty" cannot be explained without contradicting oneself. Thus, to be guilty is to confront oneself as a *reason.* I am the reason; I am the cause. The fault is mine, and the meaning of that fault is the impossibility of any other account. Guilt is ultimate. As such, it confronts being in truth fundamentally. It *is* truth.

But why must this truth be so negative? The question is as mindless as asking why pleasure must be so positive. The "no!" of guilt is as fundamental, and hence as meaningful, as the "yes" of pleasure. There is no qualification to this "yes" and this "no." It is what it means to be in truth.

It should be noted that the proper verb used in the recognition of guilt as ultimate is 'to acknowledge'. It is a familiar analysis that whatever is known is true. If I know Paris is south of London, then it is true Paris is south of London. If I say that I *know* Rome is north of London, then I have misused the term 'know'. I may *believe* this false assertion, but I cannot know it. The same logic applies to 'acknowledge'. If I acknowledge my guilt it must be true I am guilty. But if, in deception, I state that I acknowledge my guilt when in fact I am not guilty, then I have simply misused the term. In strict philosophical precision, acknowledgment states the truth of what one is rather than events or facts that occur as objects of cognition. Strictly speaking I do not acknowledge that Rome is south of Paris, unless I had previously maintained the opposite and am now admitting my error. By the same reasoning we should not say "I know I am guilty" unless the point is the purely formal one that my guilt is now being considered solely as an item of epistemic verification; that is, my guilt, like the geographical position of Rome in relation to Paris, is something which I can assert as an item of my cognition. Normally, then, to acknowledge is to establish as true some way of being which belongs to my existence. I might acknowledge being in love or in debt, and unless I am deceiving the listener by misusing the term, such acknowledgment establishes the truth of this modality. It is therefore neither a *descriptive* truth nor a *performative* utterance, but rather lies somewhere between the two. It is similar to performative uses of language because to acknowledge my guilt, for example, may mean to accept for the first time my *being* guilty; but it is also similar to descriptive uses, since my being guilty does not depend on my acknowledging it. (I may, for example, be engaged in self-deception, and hence deny my guilt, until my own awareness reveals my deception, at which time I then acknowledge my guilt.) Acknowledgment is peculiarly about my own existence, but like knowledge it necessarily entails truth.

Being guilty clearly presents us with ultimacy. Guilt cannot be accounted for by prior conditions, for then there would be no responsibility at all; and in the acknowledgment of it no appeal can be made beyond it, nor can it be escaped. To be guilty is to be in truth. It is ultimate.

Though guilt is ultimate, its opposite is not; yet curiously this opposite provides us with a greater resource for understanding the truth of guilt than the analysis of guilt itself. Existentially speaking, the opposite of guilt is not innocence, for innocence is possible only if I am first able to be guilty. To find the opposite of guilt one must reach to a far more fascinating phenomenon.

Forgiveness

To acknowledge guilt is to confront the truth as ultimate, of which it seems there can be no counter. Forgiveness, however, in no way denies my guilt, but actually transcends it by rendering guilt no longer unanswerable. Thus forgiveness cannot *deny* guilt—since as ultimate nothing outranks it—but it can transcend it. Forgiveness must not be confused either with excusing, which merely mitigates, or with justification, which demands that guilt never was present at all. Only the guilty can be forgiven, but since guilt is an ultimate terminus, forgiveness must simply establish an entirely separate and higher realm of meaning. Forgiveness, however, is itself *not* an ultimate terminus, simply because it is meaningful to ask *why* someone is forgiven, whereas it is not meaningful to ask why someone is guilty. (Of course, I *can* ask why someone *believes* another to be guilty, but here the "why" is concerned with evidence and not with the existential ground of being guilty.) It seems obvious, then, that forgiveness is made possible by the truth of guilt but is not explained by guilt. How then are we to make sense of forgiveness?

Suppose I have morally offended someone who is close to me. The guilt is absolute, as all guilt is. I deserve censure; and let us assume that, in acknowledging my guilt, I accept the need of punishment to reestablish justice. But I am forgiven. Why? Here the difference between forgiveness and guilt is palpable. I cannot ask why I am guilty, for no explanation is as adequate as the guilt itself. But to be forgiven almost demands the further question: Why? Why am I forgiven?

The "I" again is spotlighted. In guilt the "I" is revealed as fundamental. There is, however, a universality inherent in the moral law; it is *always* morally wrong to offend another as I have done. But forgiveness *cannot* be universal. Therefore, whatever it is about *me* that accounts for my being forgiven is nontransferable and completely particular. My guilt is unique; no one else can share my responsibility; but the law that determines my act as immoral is universal. In being forgiven, however, there is no universality at all. One cannot establish a universal code telling who should forgive whom and under what conditions. To forgive is always an entirely gratuitous act. So when I ask what it is about *me* that makes my forgiveness possible I cannot answer the question by reference to *what* I am. Rather, I can only answer the question by reference to *who* I am.

Whom do we forgive, and why? We forgive those we love or admire or those whom we consider to matter in a way that elevates them beyond mere membership in the species of morally responsible agents. Forgiveness is possible because I matter in some way other than my moral conduct. I am guilty for what I have *done,* I am forgiven for who I *am.* If I am the beloved son of a doting parent, my being a son transcends the guilt which I must acknowledge. Since I do not *deserve* to be forgiven and yet I *do* deserve my guilt, the language of deserving and merit is quite literally *violated* when I am forgiven.

Since I have no *right* to be forgiven, forgiveness must be seen as a bestowal. But it is a bestowal which needs a ground, and that ground is my own unique existential worth. It opposes the unique *moral* worth which is accounted for by my guilt. Thus, the unique moral worth grounded in my guilt opposes the unique existential worth which grounds forgiveness. Since forgiveness is grounded but guilt grounds, the latter alone confronts truth as ultimate.

Is it possible to reject forgiveness? Obviously not, since it does not come from me, but from the bestowing agent who in forgiving ranks who I am above what I have done. But guilt is more than what I have done; it is also the acknowledgment of the fundamental negation that burdens with its oppression. It is not merely that I have broken a promise, perceived as an *act,* it is also the irresistible acknowledgment of my negativity. Forgiveness affirms what is denied in guilt. It is the counterechoing "yes" which opposes and transcends the fundamental "no."

But if we define guilt as one of the four faces of truth, does this imply that forgiveness is a kind of falsity? We must not reject this suggestion too quickly. After all, to forgive is to cheat justice. Those who piously think that they are morally superior because they are willing to forgive are deeply self-deceived. The forgiver, for the sake of the forgiven, simply bears the terrible burden of cheating justice, and this is possible only for the truly noble. It should be clear that to "overlook" a wrong, or to "wink at transgressions," is completely alien to true forgiveness. What many consider to be forgiveness is merely a spineless lack of will to honor the guilty by accepting their responsibility. Justice is a lacerated victim of these pseudo-forgivers.

The logic is simple. To forgive is to sacrifice justice on the altar of existential worth. To be forgiven is to be loved or honored because of who one is, and this establishes an autonomous and transcending realm which burdens in its violation of justice. The pseudo-forgiver insults the wrongdoer by denying him the right to redress his own offense. In this way, the pseudo-forgiver burdens the offender by *trivializing* his unique moral worth, thereby rendering him incapable of expiation. But the true forgiver takes the burden of expiation on himself. To forgive in the true sense is therefore to become guilty for the sake of the forgiven. How are we to make sense of this?

We must be very careful in this analysis, for the language of both guilt and forgiveness is fraught with deception and dangerous enchantment. It is tempting, for example, to say that a mother forgives her son because of love. Being beloved is therefore a ground for being forgiven. Who the son is outranks what the son has done, therefore the loving mother forgives, and forgiveness is seen as a kind of transmoral loving. This is an attractive account, and there is doubtless some truth in it. But we have seen that any suspension of censure which consists in *trivializing* the dignity of guilt is merely a form of *overlooking* the demands of justice and demeaning the authenticity of guilt. The formal terminology sounds adequate; but it is too glib. For love is not noble when, as a satisfying emotion, it cancels the very foundation of dignity by treating guilt as something to be *dismissed*. In dismissing guilt one dismisses the self, and with the erasure of the self, the capacity to *matter at all* is also forfeit. The true forgiver does indeed affirm the autonomous worth of *who* the forgiven is. But in so doing the moral demand for expiation cannot entirely be dismissed. The truly loving mother, in forgiving the offending son, *suffers;* she cannot take the son's guilt upon herself, for that is impossible, since, as we have seen, guilt is ultimate and hence nontransferable. But she can embrace the expiation, demanded by justice. As long as the mother yields to the *sentiment* of avoiding the grim necessity of witnessing her son's deserved punishment, she is not a forgiver but a pseudo-forgiver. And in this there is no *truth.* There is only one quality which determines true forgiving, when the dignity of guilt and the acceptance of expiation transcend the moral, and that is nobility.

It becomes obvious, then, that the notion of 'nobility' is an important factor in distinguishing the true forgiver from the false forgiver. It is also clear that if we *understand* the appeal that a mother forgives her son because she loves him, then whatever it is about the son that accounts for his being beloved is crucial in understanding how the ultimacy of guilt is somehow avoided by the transcendence of forgiveness. This leads us to the final of the four faces of truth.

Beauty

When Romeo first spies Juliet across the dance floor he is moved to protest: "Beauty, for use, too rich; for earth, too dear." This poetic insight finds considerable philosophical support. Kant, in the *Critique of Judgment,* argues exactly the same way, insisting that aesthetic judgments cannot have a purpose. Plato, Schopenhauer, Nietzsche, Heidegger, and countless other philosophers of the highest rank have all maintained similar doctrines supporting this insight. If someone looks at a painting by Cézanne of apples on a table, and is moved to hunger, and thereby accounts for the value of the painting as an advertisement for the fruit industry, we consider him to have entirely missed the point. We do not ask what the *Pietà* is *for;* nor do we ask what we can *do* with the "Tempest Sonata." Beauty is, quite simply, too rich for use.

And yet this nonpurposive quality of beauty is rarely probed to its full meaning. For it is not merely a minor characteristic of beauty that it need not be used; rather it is a profound and fundamental quality of the very essence of beauty that it not be thought either in terms of its purpose or in terms of its cause. Beautiful things are, of course, caused; and they may even have purposes; but to think of them *as* beautiful is to think of them without reference to their cause or purpose. And of course this is the remarkable turn which is so revealing and which, in part, seems to account for our continued amazement in the face of beauty — namely, that we *can* think nonpurposively and noncausally about our experiences *at all.* For the point must be emphasized: we do *think* in the face of beauty; we do not merely feel. It is also a peculiarity of our confrontations with beauty that what is felt and what is thought seem curiously the same. Kant uses the language of 'harmony', claiming that in an aesthetic experience what is thought is in complete harmony with what is felt; but the isomorphism seems more immediate than that. It almost seems that, in the confrontation of beauty, thought and sense have become one. Plato seems to prefer this language of identity rather than harmony, for he argues that beauty is both thought and sensed at once; and indeed he suggests that this identity of thought with sense can occur *only* in the case of beauty.

Whatever reasons these diverse thinkers have for spotting beauty both as nonpurposive and as somehow unifying thought with sense, it seems clear that their insights do express a fairly universal understanding. We do not ask for the causes or the purposes of beautiful things simply because their being beautiful is enough; we seem to unify our thinking with our sensing in the confrontation of beauty because beauty needs no further justification. Even though beauty is sensed, sensing seems inadequate to account for beauty, and so we insist that it is also thought. But thinking by itself does not seem adequate to account for beauty either, so we insist it also be sensed. Yet, not wishing to distinguish between beauty as thought and beauty as sensed, we break all our previous rules and simply unify them.

This is not as cavalier as it may at first seem. All the philosophers mentioned take great pains to distinguish thought from sense in every other human activity. What is sensed is contingent, what is thought is necessary. Thought is analytic, sense is synthetic. Thought requires a mind, sense requires a body. The entire philosophical apparatus depends on the importance of this distinction. Yet in beauty the distinction is either overcome or at least greatly minimized. We are reluctant to understand beauty solely as a kind of pleasure, thus we hesitate to explain it merely as a kind of sensing; but we are also reluctant to conceive of beauty as a mere cognitive act, and therefore we hesitate to account for it merely as thought. We have seen that it is possible to learn from a great painting just what it means to see; hence in the confrontation of beauty there is something *learned* in the very seeing of it. This leads Plato to affirm a unity of sense and thought in the realization of beauty.

But if beauty is both nonpurposive *and* a unity of thought and sense, this explains why we see it as ultimate. What is learned as it is sensed provides us with truth as ultimate. A magnificent fugue by J. S. Bach is not the *result* of the laws of the fugue, rather the laws of fugue are actually *heard* in the genius of Bach's music. There is no way a purely cognitive system of rules can determine that these sounds will please. Rather like the tragic inevitability revealed *after* the story is told, the lawlikeness of the music must be heard in the music and not conceptually figured out in advance by the mind. So in the confrontation of beauty we seek no further beyond what is thoughtfully sensed, and to that extent beauty is ultimate.

Even if we grant this, however, one might protest that although beauty is indeed ultimate, why is it *true?* Perhaps it is merely ultimate as a thoughtful experience. But this is not adequate. The beauty of the Rembrandt reveals what it means to see at all, and this revelation of meaning, particularly insofar as it is ultimate, is not merely delightful or pleasant, it is truth. Whatever grounds our understanding of something is being in truth.

The search is for the right verb. Do we 'experience' beauty, or 'confront' it, or possibly even 'acknowledge' it? None of these verbs is improper or wrong, but then neither is any entirely adequate. It is revealing to consider another candidate: to 'submit' to beauty. This verb suggests that there is a power in beauty, a force which enthralls. We know it is not impossible for a man to become enslaved by the beauty of a woman, or even for a person to be enslaved by the beauty in a nonpersonal thing. It is tempting to suggest that the first of these is really only an enslavement to lust, in which the simple strength of the desire for venereal pleasure is so overwhelming that it dominates all other persuasions and renders the man a slave to his desires. This analysis may, of course, be true enough in some cases. But the notion that it is beauty and not merely desire that enslaves cannot be entirely disregarded. It is extremely difficult to tear our eyes away from a truly magnificent object of beauty regardless of the carnal excitation which may or may not accompany it. And if it is true that we can be captive to beauty and not merely to the pleasures it offers, then the consequences are remarkable. For by what authority does beauty deprive us of our will? On what warrant does it arrest the continuing development of interest, depriving us of the liberty to look away?

It may be possible to account for this empirically—that is, simply as a certain kind of psychological response to certain stimuli, the way a mongoose is excited by a cobra. But this does not seem to be the way we think about the arrests of beauty. Of course, *any* reductionist fallacy will improperly allow one kind of description to be rendered intelligible by another kind. The point is that such reductionism always leaves something out, and in the case of psychological reductionism of our involvement with beauty, a great deal appears to be left out. And so we return to the question: by what authority does beauty confront us with an ultimate arrest?

The authority is truth. There may be false or illusive things that are lovely, and beauty may often be deceptive. But in captivating our eyes, the hegemony of beauty reveals the truest meaning of seeing; we are compelled to acknowledge or submit that this beautiful object or person is why we have eyes to see in the first place, and hence to look away is inconsistent with being able to look at all. I cannot say I have really seen until beauty has ensnared my eyes. This is a *submission* or *subservience* to what is beautiful by the thinking perceiver, and in this submission one is arrested by the power or warrant of truth. Why truth? Because in the bondage to beauty we confront the ultimate.

This is the coherent explanation of the famous but puzzling identifications of truth with beauty which we encountered in Chapter 1. Why does Keats find on the Grecian urn the identification of truth with beauty? Why does Dickinson entomb the lovers of truth and beauty in a common crypt? Not because whatever is beautiful is always true, for that is ridiculous; nor because whatever is true is always beautiful, for that flies in the face of most experience. Rather, it is because the *confrontation* of beauty brings us up to what is ultimate, that is, what cannot be further explained, and to confront the ultimate is what being in truth means.

The phrase 'being in truth' does not mean having knowledge (though it might mean searching for knowledge, or at least believing that knowledge matters), nor does it mean being correct. It means rather being *able* to let truth, in the sense of confronting essence as the source of meaning, happen. Precisely because beauty *forces* us to see, and indeed to see *as essence,* can it be understood as a face of truth. To be arrested by beauty on the warrant of truth is *not to be able to look away.* On the other hand, not to be able to look at all would be the existential opposite of beauty, and it is to this concept that we must turn to complete our understanding of the fourth and last face of truth.

The Obscene

That from which we turn our face, that which, in Greek drama, took place "off the stage," is what is meant by the obscene. It does not mean the ugly, for we can look at the ugly and even be fascinated with it. Nor does it mean the pornographic, for that may well incite us to look when we should not. It does not even mean the repulsive, although this term is far closer than the others, for repulsiveness may merely be due to inexperience or upbringing. A trained physician may see the mutilated body at an auto accident not as repulsive, but as demanding his professional skills. The sensitive child, however, may be unable to face the harsh scene, and so may turn away.

The 'obscene', therefore, designates more of a formal notion than an empirical one. It is not so much that from which we *do* turn our face, for that is not universal, nor does it mean that from which we *ought* to turn our face, for that could mean an improper violation of privacy, or even pornography. Rather, the term 'obscene' means that which is *thought* as unworthy of being seen.

"Do not look upon this!" is an injunction in many myths. To look upon the head of Medusa is a fatal misadventure. Lot's wife turned into a pillar of salt when she looked upon the destruction of Sodom and Gomorrah. That certain things (mysteries) should not be known or looked at seems to entail a certain sense of sacredness. But the obscene is simply that which, when we look at it, offends the looking. Just as beauty captivates our seeing so that we cannot look away, and thereby reveals what it means to look at all, so the obscene rejects our seeing so that we cannot look at all. In exactly the same way as a contradiction both *offends* thought and *cannot be* thought, so the obscene offends seeing and thus is inconsistent with what makes us see at all.

From what, then, *do* we turn our face? If it is not the grisly or the ugly or the repulsive or the pornographic, what is it? The mythical warnings suggested above give us a clue. We turn our face away from the violation of the sacred. We do not turn away from a cruel disfigurement of a beautiful child because we are squeamish or cowardly, but because to look at such a sacrilege seems almost to *approve* of it. To look upon this heinous act is to render it worthy of being looked at. There is something so thoroughly evil about this kind of sacrilege that to confront it seems false. And so to avoid this association with the false, we do not confront it: we turn away. The language here has led us full circle. We do not confront the false—that is the rejection inherent in obscenity. This seems to suggest that what *is* confronted is truth. But this suggestion is meaningful only if by 'false' we mean the opposite of 'being in *truth*' and not merely the opposite of the true as in true sentences. We *do* confront false sentences; they are as meaningful as true ones. But if by truth is meant the source of meaning found in essence, then the false would indeed be the obscene.

But this reflection has brought us almost to the threshold of the sacred, which would take us beyond the limits of the present inquiry. It is enough to recognize why, throughout the discussion, we have spoken of *confronting* the ultimate. Truth is not so much seen or reasoned or spoken as confronted. What has shown this is the reflection on the obscene—that from which we turn away, that which is *not* confronted. But if the obscene turns us away, and if beauty is the existential opposite of the obscene, then in beauty we confront what is seen. But *what* is confronted in our seeing is truth. So beauty is a face of truth.

The Argument

Throughout the last two chapters the patience of the reader may have been sorely tried. This is an essay on truth, and for the last two chapters the topics of discussion and analysis have been pleasure, fate, guilt, and beauty, along with their opposites, suffering, freedom, forgiveness, and obscenity. The first four have been identified as the "faces of truth," but it seems unusually strained to identify fate, for example, as having anything to do with truth. Even if the reader has sensed a vague kind of connection between the topics of these two last chapters and the ostensive topic of this inquiry, it is only good manners if not also good sense to sketch out now what, prior to the analyses of the four faces, could not have been presented. The following is in no way meant as a logical demonstration. Rather it represents the methodological framework of an inquiry.

1. If we restrict ourselves to a purely formal description, truth becomes 'that which makes questioning intelligible'. (For unless it is possible for the door to be open it is meaningless to ask whether the door is open.)

2. To question intelligibly is to seek a response which satisfies or terminates. This satisfaction or termination of interrogation is what is meant by truth in its fundamental sense.

3. It may seem that 'satisfaction' is not enough, for false answers may 'satisfy' some questioners. But the description in #2 demands *intelligible* questioning, which asks for the correct response. For I do not want to be deceived when I ask—for the asking itself makes sense only if the response does indeed respond. *Whether* a response is correct lies beyond the inquiry into the nature and meaning of truth.

4. Satisfaction of intelligible questioning is possible only when the asking can elicit (a) affirmation, (b) acceptance, (c) acknowledgment, or (d) submission.

5. Knowledge qualifies as the intelligible satisfaction of some kinds of questions; for I can *affirm* the response as 'that which I want to know'; I can *accept* the response in recognizing that it is independent of what I want; I can *acknowledge* the response in recognizing that it is *my own* rationality and experience which reveals it to me; and I can *submit* to the response by yielding to the power or weight of evidence that demands my recognition of the response *as* true.

6. But *knowledge* is the satisfaction only of intelligible questioning about 'whether' or 'what' something is.

7. There seems to be a meaningful and legitimate usage of the term 'truth' which is not entailed in a knowledge claim.

8. This suggests a distinction between what is *true* and *truth*,

although this distinction is valid only within the inquiry; it does not seem to find support in a mere appeal to ordinary language.

9. Nevertheless, the formal provisional description in #2 remains: both the 'true' and 'truth' provide some kind of satisfaction to various forms of questions.

10. The realm of 'truth' is the realm in which the question is about the meaning found in essences. The realm of the 'true' is that in which knowledge provides terminal answers.

11. Essences, like true answers, provide a terminus. Since the strictness of the terminology is important here, it would be improper to say that one *knows* essences, for then an essence would be the same as an answer. Instead we *confront* that which needs no further explanation. We *know* what is true; we *confront* the truth.

12. There is no limit to the possible number of essences which we can confront, any more than there are limits to questions of fact which can receive terminal answers in knowledge.

13. But the confrontation of the truth of essence needs to be explained. What must be assumed about the inquirer in order to account for the possibility of confronting truth in essences?

14. The philosophical response to #13 cannot be found in any account of how we *know,* since knowledge is restricted to true answers.

15. Therefore it is necessary to interpret what it means to confront that which is not explainable by reference to anything beyond the confrontation itself. Whatever these interpretations are, they must coincide with the formal understanding of truth in #1 and #2.

16. The *confrontation* of what is not explainable beyond the limits of what is confronted can be shortened to the 'confrontation of the ultimate'. In order to 'confront the ultimate', one *must* presuppose (a) the ability to *affirm* what is ultimate; this is found in *pleasure;* (b) the ability to *accept* what is ultimate, either by being grateful for, or by the noble endurance of, what is bestowed; this is *fate;* (c) the ability to *acknowledge* what is ultimate; this is found in *guilt;* (d) the ability to *submit to* what is ultimate; this is *beauty.*

17. It is by no means odd or unusual to say that truth is that which can be affirmed, accepted, acknowledged, or submitted to. In the ordinary sense of true answers, one also affirms, accepts, acknowledges, and submits to what is true (cf. #5).

18. This analysis has merely interpreted these four responses to truth in nonepistemic terms. That is, it has shown what it means to accept, affirm, acknowledge, and submit when one is *not* speaking of *knowledge,* but still speaks of truth.

19. The four faces of truth, then, are the necessary *existential* (rather than epistemic) presuppositions of truth. Since we cannot speak of a subject which *knows* what is true, we must speak simply of 'being in truth'. Since that which satisfies the questioner can and must do so only if the questioner can affirm, accept, acknowledge, and submit, this analysis has rendered a nonarbitrary and consistent interpretation of what it means to be in truth.

20. In all cases of confronting the ultimate I cannot and do not *decide whether* I will confront; the confrontation is independent of my decisions or will.

21. Thus there is nothing arbitrary or subjective about the confrontation of the ultimate. For if by 'ultimate' is meant 'that which cannot be explained or accounted for beyond itself', then no subjective or arbitrary condition of the questioner will qualify as an account.

22. Knowledge, of course, does *not* presuppose the four faces of *truth;* for knowledge is of the *true.*

23. Confrontation of the ultimate, as well as the search for essence, is impossible for anyone incapable of pleasure, fate, guilt, and sensitivity to beauty. It is therefore logically possible, though empirically unlikely, that one could have knowledge and thereby know what is true, but *not* confront essential ultimacy, and hence lack the truth.

24. In both the search for knowledge and the confrontation of truth there is no guarantee of success. Both the knowledge-seeker and the essence-seeker may be beguiled or deceived. But there exist canons of verification as well as procedures of testing which, though not infallible, nevertheless save the enterprise from a hopeless uncertainty. Obviously at

any time I can be mistaken about whether I have knowledge; and I can likewise fail to understand the essential meaning of a question of truth. But neither of these possibilities implies scepticism in the case of the true or nihilism in the case of truth. The discovery *that* I was at one time deceived, or *that* I had not confronted the essential truth, already reveals a meaningful distinction between the true and the false on the one hand and truth and untruth on the other.

These twenty-four points constitute the "argument," that is, the justification for the analysis of the two previous chapters. It must be reiterated that pleasure, fate, guilt, and beauty do not always provide *knowledge*, that pleasure, for example, may lead us astray. Rather, the four faces reveal what must be presupposed about us if we are able to be in truth at all. They also reveal why truth matters. But this is by no means obvious; and the question deserves an independent section.

PART FOUR
THE WORLD

9

The World

Whatever else is required in our understanding of truth, surely it must be asked in what way the world plays a role in our account. For an inquiry into truth which did not consider the world would surely be so alien to our normal understanding as to be unworthy of serious reflection. 'The way the world is' seems, indeed, to be what most people in ordinary speaking mean when they use the word 'truth'. And even if this vague identification cannot sustain the rigor of a philosophical critique, it nevertheless suggests that somehow, in some way, an adequate account of truth must include the role played by the world we live in. If truth is described independently of the world, we may rightly suspect that such a description is so abstract, so intellectualistic or purely cognitive, that the entire endeavor has simply been blinded by a false light. To understand truth is to understand, in part, what is meant by the world.

This cannot be denied. However, exactly *how* the notion of the world fits into the understanding of truth is by no means obvious or clear. Much of the obfuscation concerning this question is due to the philosophical tradition which initiates all of its inquiries from the position of an isolated knowing subject—the Enlightenment. Before the present inquiry can successfully analyze the role that the meaning of the world plays in our understanding of truth, it is necessary first to expunge the harmful influence of the epistemic prejudice in raising the question. Enlightenment thinkers have provided us with an inheritance which focuses attention almost exclusively on the mind when the question of truth is concerned, just as they focus almost exclusively on the individual and his rights when the question is of political or social significance. This focus on the knowing subject and the individual agent is profoundly onerous, and must be carefully exposed so that its anesthetizing opiate can be isolated and excised.

Kant, who represents both the culmination and the surpassing of all such thinking, left as a philosophical legacy a remarkable and powerful form of questioning, which he took to be the most fundamental way of addressing all great problems in philosophy: "What must be presupposed about the human mind if x is possible?" X could be any philosophically interesting activity whatsoever, such as mathematics, science, morality, or even aesthetic judgment. "How is mathematics possible?" he asked; and his answer was: because the human mind is designed to *do* mathematics. This inheritance has served us in some ways remarkably well, and under the influence of this legacy considerable philosophical wealth is provided. But for all its indubitable value, it remains a mentalist approach, and consequently leaves much that is precious unconsidered.

It was not always this way. The ancient Greeks seemed to recognize the need to ask both questions. In their search for an understanding of love, for example, they asked not only about the various passions of the lover, but also about the singular quality which provoked the passions in the first place: beauty. The longing of the lover *together with* the beauty of the beloved provides us with a superior understanding of love. For the Enlightenment, the known is approached through the knower, a curious strategy indeed, since it seems to support the very scepticism which the thinkers of the period were endeavoring to thwart. As soon as a thinker entertains the idea of a knowing mind confronted with the external world which is to be known, the gap created by this approach is already unbridgeable. For, almost without realizing it, the thinker instinctively assumes *a mind which is not in the world,* and *a world which lies outside the mind.* A glance at any text of Enlightenment or even contemporary epistemology will reveal this unfortunate and misological approach. Totally absurd questions, such as "How can the knowing mind ever be guaranteed access to the external world?" are asked in all seriousness. But such a question cannot be answered, and a fatal scepticism or a naive realism follows. The question itself is at fault, for it *assumes* a disjunction between mind and world which simply cannot be thought without contradiction. If there is such a thing as a mind, it must be in the world; and if there is such a thing as the world, it already contains the mind. The mind, as part of the world, cannot step out of the world and achieve an independence, as a state might secede from a union. Nor can the world ever be "external" to the mind, as an outlaw is external to society. To be sure, epistemic errors are possible, but they are not due to the alienation of the mind from the world. Errors, as well as proper and correct judgments, are of minds within the world, and can be recognized *as* errors only because of this.

It is a curiosity that many sceptics begin with an awareness that we make errors: If I have erred in the past, there is no way I can be assured I am not in error *now,* and any real knowledge is impossible. But this argument is absurd, for it depends upon the inference that the possibility of error is inconsistent with knowledge, when in fact the opposite inference is the only valid one. In order to *have* error—and by this I mean that I can discover that I was originally mistaken about something— I must first be able to distinguish what is true from what is false. How did I ever learn that my original belief was mistaken? The *recognition* of error assumes a further recognition of the canons by which errors can be recognized and in some cases righted. That I may *now* be in error merely shows that knowledge is not dependent on the *now,* not that knowledge is altogether impossible. Further, recognition of prior error is *knowledge:* I cannot assert I was wrong unless I know that what I believed previously was incorrect. What this means is that error does not separate me from the world, but rather is a part of being in the world. If error were to make any certain knowledge impossible the result would be total and complete belief, ever unaware that *any* error had been made.

What is at stake is the false doctrine that the mind and the world are two separated entities, somehow mysteriously *bridged* by a vague and uncertain relation. With such a starting point one is reduced either to a numbing scepticism or to a nihilistic empiricism in which knowledge is restricted to the correct and critical usage of the empirical faculties, which can only provide us with what is the case, that is, with the simple occurrence of events in nature (facts). Moral, aesthetic, spiritual, and religious ideas are thereby reduced to mere beliefs with no ground in reality, and thus become "subjective." But the "subject" is, after all, real enough: it is part of the world. And so the severe separation of mind from world presupposed by this doctrine is refuted by it. In spite of this, the insidious error continues to attract and ensnare many clever people.

The mind/world disjunction, so lethal for the problem of knowledge, is even more deadly in the attempt to understand truth. For under the persuasion of this false doctrine, "truth," without any independent metaphysical status, is assigned the impossible task of bridging the gap between a thing-dominated world and an idea-dominated mind. It is seen as a mere relation between unrelatable things, and to make matters

worse, its genesis and environment are restricted to mysterious propositions embedded in sentences. Surely, then, if a meaningful existential
account of truth is to succeed, the notion of the *world* must be reconsidered.

But how can we talk about 'world' except as the external reservoir of
the causes of our sensations? If 'world' is *not* the final metaphysical
referent, how can it be thought? It was noted above that mind must
always be understood as already being in the world. This means that
'world' must be understood at the very least as that *in which* the mind *is*,
though not, as we shall see, simply as another entity alongside other
things like lakes and squirrels. The mind, too, must be rethought as
belonging *within* the world, and not as some transcendent perspective
outside it. If we take these two insights together we see that being in the
world is a necessary existential condition for mind, and containing or
enclosing the mind is a necessary existential condition for world. But
these discoveries require that neither 'mind' nor 'world' be thought as
entities. For whatever is an entity must be within the world, and the
world cannot be within itself; and if mind is a necessary condition for
world it cannot be an entity within the world and certainly not an entity
outside of the world. To be in the world is a way of being or existence,
and to be or to exist is to be in the world. What is significant about this
argument is that the language of entities is here replaced by the language of modality or ways of being.

To exist is necessarily *already* to be in the world, therefore the world
is a *modality* of our existence which *must* be presupposed. To be in the
world is thereby an a priori modality, and all reference to an entity
"mind" and another entity "world" falls away. Truth is one of the ways
we find ourselves being in the world. The task is therefore not the
impossible one of linking up two separated entities with a purely rela-
tional chain, but simply to understand 'world' in such a way as to let
truth matter. There must be something about being in the world that
accounts for both what is true and truth. When we speak of the world
with regard to what is true, we think of the world as making what is true
possible, but in speaking of the world with regard to truth, we think of
the world as that which makes truth *matter*. What makes the true possible is the world seen as *actuality*; what makes truth matter is the world
seen as *reality*. The real is the ground of truth, the actual is the ground of
the true. That the world, either as actuality or as reality, is the ground of
the true and truth is an ancient doctrine as well as an intuitive, common-
sense one; it is defended, for example, by Plato in the *Republic*.

The question now can be asked more precisely: how must we think about what 'world' means if it is to render being in truth meaningful? If truth is to matter, what must the world be like? With the dreadful distortions provided by the Enlightenment thinkers now spotted and hopefully revealed as erroneous, it is possible to raise this question properly.

The fourfold character of being in truth was revealed in the previous section as affirmation, acceptance, acknowledgment, and submission. These four ways of being in truth can now be used to guide us in the inquiry into what the world must be like if truth is to matter. This procedure does not, however, reflect any mere slavishness to symmetry or form, although it should not be surprising that there might be an isomorphism between 'being in truth' and 'what makes truth matter'. What follows is an account of what being in the world must mean if truth is to matter. Or to be philosophically precise: an account of how we must *think* about the world if truth is to be possible and to matter.

1. First, the world must be thought as having a history. This means more than that the world is in time, or even that it has a past. For a history is a *story,* and as a story its meaning *unfolds* in the narrative form. Of course, it may seem obvious or even trivial that the world has a history (or "*is* historical," if the verbal form of 'being' is preferred). But the story of the world is no ordinary story; rather it is the ultimate story—that unfolding of narrative meaning which is fundamental, and which makes all other stories possible. To say that the world is historical is to say that being in the world is made intelligible by the unfolding of the ultimate *as* a story. To be in the world is therefore to partake in the unfolding or revealing of narrative meaning. It is not the different events that make up history, rather it is history that makes the events. For an event *is* an event only because of its occurrence *within* the unfolding of a tale. But since this is the ultimate tale (that is, it is not made intelligible by something else), it is what we mean by 'world'.

2. On an even more intuitive level, by 'world' we also mean where we belong. The world is our home. It is not first a place which then becomes familiar, rather it is first our home, and only after this realization does it take on the character of place. Since it is ultimate, the world is not *a* place (for whatever is a place is a place in the world), but rather the necessary condition or possibility of there being places at all. The world makes places possible; but it is first a source of belonging. Now,

we speak of belonging *in a place*, but the world, not being *a* place but the possibility of all places, is thus the origin of our belonging (or *not* belonging) at all. Thus, the world is both ours and not ours; it is that from which we are estranged and for which we yearn in homesickness. It is a peculiarity that thinking seems, in many ways, to be the culprit in our estrangement from the world, for the less reflective we are, the more familiar we are in our belonging in the world. On the other hand, to be thoughtless is to be unaware of the very possibilities of alienation and belonging. But whether we are thoughtful or thoughtless, the world is for us a home, from which we have been estranged or in which we are familiar.

3. The third existential sense of world which makes truth matter is the role it plays in providing our existence with some sense of success or failure. The world is the ultimate *tribunal* in which the story becomes a testimonial, and the worth of existence is weighed. The ability to think of our existence as failing or succeeding—however vague and imprecise this judgment may be—requires the world. For unless the world can provide the basis for assessing the worth of existence, it cannot matter to be at all. Phrases such as "to matter" and "to succeed or fail" are not evaluations by some worldless subject (and hence are not "subjective") but are rather about the world *as* the world. In other words, what matters matters *in* the world *because* of the world. "To matter" is to be in the world in truth. When we speak in the colloquial way, saying, "but does it *really* matter?" the appeal is to *reality,* which is the world grounding truth. Thus we belong to a world—or are alienated from a world—which is a tribunal or fundamental basis for judgment as well as a home. Indeed it may well be that the ultimate judgment of the world as tribunal just is about our belonging or our alienation.

4. The final meaning of the world as the ground of truth is that it beckons. The world is the ultimate and fundamental lure, that *Ewige Weibliche* which *leads* us, as the beauteous beloved seduces the lover, the cream entices the cat, the magnet pulls the iron. But in beckoning, the world does not promise beyond itself, as if there were a further reason or reward which prompted us to seek and serve. Rather, by 'world' is meant that which itself is active, dynamic, full of life and change, and thus lures us to itself because of its own favors. The world is the tragic carnival, whose lights, sounds, smells, and bustle attract the wayward first with innocent glee and then with somber inevitability, but always as a beckoning, a call to join or belong, the lure of the resting place for the

burdened and weary. The world, in other words, is the desired just because of its reality; it seduces because of the ennui of the false, the emptiness of the illusory. To be in truth is to be vulnerable to the siren call of reality. To say we are *led* is to recognize the world as the ultimate beckoning.

These four meanings of 'world' correspond to the four ways of being in truth: (1) I *accept* the inevitable unfolding of the fated story; (2) I *affirm* the world as the home I enjoy; (3) I *acknowledge* my guilt in the world as tribunal; and (4) I *submit* to the allure and seduction of the world, as a lover submits to beauty. This symmetry, however, should not be overly stressed. Its appeal is to show that the inquiry is consistent and orderly. But the full force of these four aspects of the world cannot be grasped merely from the preceding list. Subsequent chapters will develop these themes more fully. Nevertheless, the symmetry does have significance, and before proceeding to the richer existential analyses of these themes, it may prove beneficial to reconsider how this inquiry into *truth* has yielded such remarkable fruit.

Let us assume the door is open, and I, sitting with my back to it, feel a draft, and ask: "Is the door open?" My companion, sitting vis-à-vis me, can see the door, and answers: "Yes, the door is open." We say: what makes this sentence *true* is that it reveals the way the world actually is; and accepting it as true, I acknowledge and submit to the reasons and evidence for it being the way it is; and since, as true, the answer has provided me with what I wanted to know, I can affirm it. Thus, the true response to my question (a) is affirmed, accepted, acknowledged, and submitted to, and (b) is about the world—that is, it expresses what is actually the case. We now consider another kind of question, one which asks not *whether* something is or *what kind of thing* something is, but what it means to be in some way or situation. We ask: what does it mean to be a mother? Realizing that the identificatory "female parent" is *true,* we also recognize that the question asks for a different *kind* of response. We distinguish 'true' from 'truth', recognizing that these are *parallel* terms—that is, they are fundamentally the same, but with important philosophical differences. Because they are parallel terms, the symmetry of the analyses of the two terms is not surprising.

When we turn to the *truth* of the question about the essence or meaning of a mother, we find that, just as in the true response about the open door, there is affirmation, acceptance, acknowledgment, and submission. We also recognize that *what* we accept, affirm, acknowledge, and submit to is the unfolding of the *world*. To make the terms of the distinction both parallel and separate, we distinguish the *actual* door being *actually* open and the *real* mother being revealed as *really* forgiving beyond prudence. To be *able* to confront the truth (which is parallel to 'knowing what is true') one must be able to affirm (pleasure), to accept (fate), to acknowledge (guilt), and to submit (to beauty). Just as the *actual* open door makes the sentence "the door is open" *true*, so the *real* meaning of a mother is confronted in truth because of reality. The open door makes the true sentence *possible*, the confrontation of the essential meaning of a mother makes the truth *matter*. In order for the truth to *matter* it must (a) unfold, as a story; (b) house, as a home in which we are familiar or from which we are estranged; (c) weigh, as a tribunal judging the worth of existence; and (d) beckon, as a lure. In these four ways, the truth becomes grounded *as* (not "in") reality, and is hence in and about the *world*.

10

Truth as a Story

The world is available to us at all only because we are already *in* it, so that the world is made available, that is, revealed, only as ways of being in the world. This does not freeze us into solipsism or subjectivism, because there is no inference that others—whether people, events, or entities other than myself—in any way *depend* on my existence or my being in the world. Scepticism and nihilism might obtain if the world I seek to understand and know were *not* the same as the world in which I exist. The point is merely that such phenomena as knowing and understanding are *ways* of being in the world, though not necessarily the only ones.

One of the most fundamental ways of being in the world is that of developing, growing, learning, and changing in the great unfolding process of time. To be in the world is to be in time; and furthermore to understand oneself as being in the world, as well as to understand the world itself, is to confront the temporal unfolding of who and what we are, as well as the world we are in, as a story. For by a story is meant the unfolding development of narrative meaning by which what was past becomes meaningful in terms of what is present and what is projected in the future. If truth is historical (which is *not* to say that truth is relative to different epochs, nor is it to espouse any other form of historicism), three distinct areas of concern present themselves as important for the inquiry.

Since a story is unfolded or revealed in its telling, we must ask first about the meaning of unfolding, and second about the meaning of language as telling. And since a story requires the temporal division of a past, present, and future (or as Aristotle puts it: a beginning, a middle, and an end), the temporal structure of existence, that is, the *historical* structure of being, must also be considered. Thus truth as unfolding, truth as language, and truth as temporal become the topics of this chapter.

Truth as Unfolding

H. C. Andersen has written some of the most powerful and direct stories since Aesop, and although (or perhaps because) they are written for children, they reveal the irresistible power of the narrative structure to illuminate what things mean. In the story "The Princess and the Pea," a tale almost universally known throughout Western civilization, this illuminative structure can be spotted effortlessly. Note the way he begins: "There was once a Prince who wanted to marry a Princess; but she was to be a *real* Princess." Great novelists might envy Andersen's ability to create, in a *single sentence,* such an opening. For by his simplistic, childlike prose, he has opened the floodgate. Just by the way the sentence is written we know that not just anyone can be a princess; that indeed there is a problem between appearance and reality; that the essence of a princess is not available for the uncautious or perhaps, even, the unqueenly. We all know how the story unfolds: the prince's mother, the queen, confronts the poor, rain-drenched child who looks like a homeless and wretched waif, and places a single vegetable, a pea, beneath the stack of twenty eiderdown mattresses. The child, though exhausted, is unable to sleep well, because she can feel the lump beneath the pile of mattresses. Because of her sensitivity, the child is recognized as a *true* princess. This is how we think about princesses: not that they have power or that they are the daughters of kings, but simply that, in their sensitivity, they are special. After this one-page story, Andersen ends: "Look you, this is a *true* story." It is true not because it actually happened, as every child instinctively knows, but because it truly reveals what it means for there to be princesses. The story unfolds or uncovers what the essence of a princess is. And it does so only through the narrative form. The child is shown to be a true princess, worthy of marrying a prince, not because she can identify the royalty of her parents, but because of who she is. The story suggests, but does not state, that even if she were lowborn she would *still* be a true princess, the same way the boy Arthur is destined to be king because he extracts Excalibur from a stone. No one believes it is Arthur's physical strength that withdraws the sword: he did not become king because he had extracted the sword; rather, he could withdraw the sword because he was king.

Defining a princess as one who is too sensitive to sleep on a pile of mattresses on top of a pea does not *reveal* anything, though the definition may be *true*. Such a definition sounds silly even to a child's ear. The story must be *told*. It is the *telling* of it that reveals the truth—namely, how to think about princesses. (Indeed, the story still charms and reveals in a healthy republican democracy where actual princesses do not belong. The political is simply irrelevant. As long as this story is told, hopefully forever, in spite of antitraditionalists, feminists, Marxists, and minimalists, there will be this truth, that what is princely can be found in rain-soaked, wretched urchins; and because of this independence of the actual political order, the story remains, as its author insists, a true one.) So the telling of the story uncovers or reveals what it means to be a princess.

We are not surprised when philosophers point out that knowledge requires more than the mere belief in, or assertion of, what is the case, for one might stumble on the facts by accident or believe what is the case for the wrong reasons. And so we quite properly insist that knowledge must be supported by reasons or evidence. In a similar way, truth cannot merely be that which characterizes what is the case; it must be understood as something more than what the world is like, and that extra requirement is the manifestation or unfolding of what the world is like. This unfolding or uncovering is the essence of truth, which is why a mere *description* of a princess in terms of her sensitivity or of a mother in terms of her being a female parent is not truth, though the two descriptions may both be true.

Truth is not '*that which* unfolds or reveals', but simply the unfolding itself. Such unfolding need not be restricted to actual stories, whether fictive or historical. The unfolding of a philosophical inquiry also reveals as truth, as may other endeavors. Neither should one assume that *any* story or *any* inquiry will reveal as truth, for obviously some stories that appear to unfold and reveal will instead conceal and distort. But *what* stories reveal or conceal is not the *truth*, for that would separate the revealing from the truth. A false story is not one which reveals misinformation or uncovers a wrong understanding of an essence; rather, a false story is one which does not reveal at all. What makes a story false is its failure to disclose or uncover; it rather conceals or covers up.

Indeed it is possible to tell a false story which consists only of true sentences, since it is obvious that one can conceal while referring to what is the case.

The fundamental metaphor of 'unfolding' is significant because it forfeits the possibility of understanding truth as a mere static relationship between a cognitive subject and a known object. What unfolds is dynamic, and this movement is not solely the function of the inquirer, seeker, or storyteller. The world itself, whether as reality (truth) or actuality (the true), participates actively in this phenomenon of truth. The inquirer also participates, not as a passive recipient, nor as the sole activator of what happens, but as an equal participant with reality in the dynamics of truth as unfolding. This image, however, should not be taken as supporting any kind of representationalism, in which the reality of a thing or event is distinguished from its representation as appearance. Reality is unfolded in the unfolding truth; and this just means there is no difference between a 'hidden' reality and an 'unhidden' representation. To be real is to unfold, and the unfolding itself is truth.

The importance of these refinements can scarcely be overstressed. A representational theory is fundamentally unsound because it is based on an image which is unimaginable. One steps back from a supposed knower, observes the phenomenon of seeing, and argues that the knower apprehends only the image or picture of what is real. But this is to presuppose what is being proven. The word 'desk' does not refer to some abstracted metaphysical entity lurking behind the desk I use and see; nor is the desk "merely" what I see and use, since its autonomy is already built into the *way* I use it. I cannot "imagine" someone looking at a real thing but seeing only its representation, for such an image already contains *in itself* the difference between the real and the represented desk, which should be unavailable to anyone looking at the phenomenon. I am required to imagine what I have defined as unimaginable—that is, a nonrepresented desk. Thus, reality cannot be understood as some vague thing-in-itself which is somehow behind and beyond what is revealed; rather reality is *what* is revealed and truth is the revealing. This becomes clearer when we realize that truth is properly about meanings or essences and not about isolated instances of knowing.

Nevertheless, the point deserves to be further developed. We are all familiar with those who argue, if not for relativistic truth, at least for *perspectival* truth, by an appeal to the charming story of the five blind men who approach for the first time an elephant. The first blind man feels the trunk and judges the elephant to be like a large snake; the second feels a foot and judges the elephant to be like a tree; the third feels the tusk and judges the animal to be like a branch; the fourth feels the massive side and judges it to be like a wall; and the fifth, feeling the tail, judges the elephant to be like a worm. The storyteller usually appeals to this remarkable tale as a persuasion to recognize that truth is always and merely a perspective. Unfortunately the story is coherent only for those who already know what an elephant is, and only *because* of that knowledge can we judge the blind men's interpretations as comically restricted. The tale succeeds in warning us not to judge things too quickly or from a single perspective; it does *not* succeed in showing that we have *only* perspectives, for behind every claim that x is a perspective one always finds the further question: perspective *of what?* Obviously if we were limited to perspectives all five blind men would be equally correct, which would entirely deflate the significance of the story.

These reflections show that representationalism and perspectivalism are ill founded; but their main purpose is merely to show that truth happens as an unfolding of reality—that is, truth occurs as a fundamental way of being in the world. Strictly speaking, we do not see truth, we watch it—or perhaps better: we learn as it unfolds. Here the verb 'unfold' can be understood either visually, as when we watch a bud unfold into a flower, or verbally, as when we hear a tale unfold in its telling. But the main point is that truth happens as an event that reveals in the occurrence of being in the world. It is not so much a move from darkness into light, for there is nothing really dark about a bud or the first line of an unknown tale. Rather it is the metamorphosis from disinterest to interest, from the unnoticed to the remarkable. There is nothing to catch the eye when the green foliage still covers the bright crimson of the rose; but as the first cracks in the covering or sheltering growth appear, and the evocative, even alluring flash of red winks through the widening slits, the blossoming of the rose becomes an event worthy of our vision. We may have *seen* the covering growth prior to the bud breaking open, but our own seeing did not matter, except in a utilitarian way. Now, with the occurrence of the bud, we do not merely see, we *watch,* and the unfolding loveliness makes our watching matter. As the story begins our expectations are entirely nonspecific. We listen only because we remember enjoying previous stories, not because *this* story has any value. But as the story unfolds, it is precisely *this* story that gives meaning to our listening.

If the term 'inquirer' or 'philosopher' in its Greek sense is substituted for 'observer' in the case of the unfolding rose or 'listener' in the case of the unfolding story, the metaphoric parallel to truth is obvious. Just as the story is available only to the listener and the blooming only to the observer, so truth is available only to the inquirer (philosopher), though these terms must be taken in their broadest possible senses. Reality is thus not *referred to,* nor is it merely *known;* much less is it *hidden* behind some inadequate representation. Rather, reality is revealed or unfolded as being in the world.

If we carefully define our terms, we have, then, the following account. The world is reality when conceived dynamically, and its unfolding is truth; the world is actuality when conceived statically and as true. Unfolding occurs as a mode or way of being in the world, in which or through which the essence is revealed as mattering, and is available only to the philosophical inquirer in the broad sense, which means anyone who asks about the meaning of essences simply because such essences in their unfolding reveal what it means to be in the world. So 'unfolding' is the key. It and it alone makes the correlative terms—such as reality, actuality, mattering, world, knowing—possible. The confrontation of truth, in acceptance, affirmation, acknowledgment, and submission, is possible only because truth *unfolds.*

But by far the most important result of this analysis is the establishment of the *autonomy* of truth. Truth no longer is a mere servant of knowledge, nor a mere predicate of a sentence. It is not merely a different name given to the world or to reality, nor is it equated with a fact. Truth matters just because it is *not* submerged as a part of our understanding of other ideas. Because truth is the unfolding of reality it is not restricted to representations, nor is it a mere set of quotation marks around reality. It has its own unique and vital role to play in the understanding and actual confrontation of who we are and the world in which we dwell. The question "*How* does truth unfold?" takes us to the next topic.

Truth and Language

Truth unfolds in several ways, but there is one fundamental, indeed paradigmatic, way in which this happens, and the way is language.

> A sentence uttered makes a world appear
> Where all things happen as it says they do.
> We doubt the speaker, not the words we hear
> Words have no word for words that are not true.

This stanza from the poem "Words" by W. H. Auden reveals much of how we think about language. There are some deep paradoxes in this poetic quotation which deserve careful reflection and analysis, but the very use of a *poetic* quotation to initiate this brief consideration of language itself demands explanation. Why begin with a poem? If Aristotle is correct, and one should explain the complex by beginning with the simple and intuitively obvious, is not this approach backwards? Poetry may be language, but it is highly sophisticated and stylized, assuming centuries of culture and refinement. Would it not be both simpler and wiser to begin with language on its most elemental level—a series of sounds which, through custom, have come to be recognized as identifying or referring to entities? A primitive Anglo-Saxon may have grunted something like 'tree' as he pointed to an oak, and from this crude beginning the glory of English was born. Accordingly, the foundation of language seems to be referentialist communication.

As we will soon see, however, language cannot be understood as communication, at least not essentially, and it is to the essence of language and not one of its uses that this inquiry is directed. For reasons I trust will become obvious, Aristotle's method of beginning with the simple is here not applicable. To initiate the quest for the essence of language by a reflection on a master of its usage, especially when the poem is not only itself great language but *about* language, is not entirely inappropriate.

The very first line reveals prodigious insight. We must note, however, that Auden tells us that a sentence makes *a* world appear (not *the* world), and further, the poet does *not* say that a sentence *creates* a world. By using the indefinite article the poet reveals that language produces the appearance of a world in the sense of a domain of relevance and intelligibility. Without language we would have no sense of the term 'world' at all. What does this mean? Auden does not say that "a sentence uttered" makes individual objects or entities appear, for that would endow language with metaphysically creative powers, which is absurd. Obviously our use of language does not mean that things like trees and lakes pop into existence by magic. It is not the trees and lakes that appear because of language, but the world in which these entities belong and interrelate. Now this is puzzling and profound. A world is precisely that which does *not* appear to us, in the normal sense. Things or objects that are *in* the world appear to us, but the world itself, which can never be *seen* in its entirety, can scarcely be said to appear. Yet, in language, the isolated and disconnected entities are given a *place*, "a local habitation and a name"; they are, because we talk about them, seen as parts of a coherent whole which itself is not a perceived object but a realm of thinkability. Language, therefore, while not creating either the objects or the world, nevertheless reveals a world as an intelligible notion for the first time. Without language there would be no world revealed or made available to us, since neither 'the world' nor 'a world' can be perceived by any faculty whatsoever. 'World' can only be presupposed or conceived, but these mental activities themselves require some sense of language. The line means further that the *way* we speak, or even the specific language we speak, such as English or German, influences the way we think about our environment. A harsh, guttural command in German lets a militant world of authority and power appear; a soft, seductive whisper in French may let a sensual world of delightful decadence appear. Thus, it is not the existence of objects that appears in the use of language, but that which makes these objects meaningful: a world.

The poet carefully assures us that the sentence makes a world *appear*. Here the emphasis again is placed on meaning rather than brute existence. 'To appear' does not mean 'to come into existence', but to be made visible or sensible. The suggestion is that the world is already there, waiting to be uncovered, the way a hidden intention appears in the unfolding of a plot. The point is *not* that language deals with mere appearance as opposed to reality, but simply that language makes available to us the already existing reality which prior to language remained unavailable. This 'availability' is appearance, which *only* language can provide.

The poem carefully avoids granting to the users of language any guarantee. There is, after all, doubting. But, we learn from the poem, what is doubted is the *speaker*, not the words. Words obviously can be abused; indeed the power to deceive is itself made possible by language. But the fault is not language itself, but the ignorance or guile of those who use it. If language is the source of lying, so too must it be the source of correcting the lie, so that words remain our only hope of extracting ourselves from ignorance. Hence, according to the poet, words have no word for what is not true.

The stanza's ending with the term 'true' is highly significant. The point of language is not its many possible uses, such as communicating, warning, commanding, informing, deceiving, swearing, lying, and promising, for it is possible to imagine many of these activities performed nonlinguistically. Rather, the point of language is truth. "Words have no word for words that are not true" obviously does not mean that whatever is spoken is true, it means that words themselves (that is, language) are our best, and perhaps only, resource for truth. This tells us almost as much about truth as it does about language, and the reasoning deserves analysis.

We are told by the professors that language is a form of communication, and from these pedants we also learn that as a means of communication, language is at best third-rate. Apparently the statistical surveys show that nonverbal communication is far more successful than language. A student retains only ten percent of what is read in a book or heard in a lecture, thirty percent of what is shown on television, fifty percent of what is witnessed, and eighty percent of what is learned by participation. Thus it seems obvious that language is not *needed* to communicate at all. Primitive people can grunt and point, thereby making their wants and needs known quite well without language; modern people apparently communicate more successfully through body language (a fascinating metaphor!) and gestures than through well-spoken sentences. We are all familiar with that pearl of Chinese wisdom to the effect that one picture is worth a thousand words.

The wisdom of these surveys is often overlooked. There can be no doubt that by bashing you over the head with a club I communicate to you that I am angry better than by merely saying so; and there is even less doubt that one photograph of a lion devouring a zebra depicts immediately more blood and gore than a good writer could achieve in three or four thousand words. But these examples merely show us that language does not communicate certain kinds of things very well. Perhaps the description of language *as* mere communication is at fault.

Kant has an ingenious argument concerning reason and happiness that provides us with an enlightening analogy. Reason, he says—quite accurately—is a lousy faculty for making us happy. By far the happiest are those who do not reason at all; if one wants to be happy the best faculties are the instincts, for they are *designed* to make us happy. Reason seems peculiarly well suited to achieve the opposite, for the more I think and wonder, the further I remove myself from my instincts, and accordingly the further I am removed from being happy. Kant's conclusion is so obvious it almost makes us smile: reason is not designed to make us happy; rather its purpose is to make us worthy of being happy.

A similar approach may be taken with language. Language may be a third-rate communicator, but it is first-rate in revealing truth. As a communicator, the Chinese picture is indeed worth a thousand words, but as an unfolder of truth, not a thousand pictures can equal a single English word.

Language as an unfolding of truth, however, can never be understood if one depicts this existential phenomenon in terms of its origin in a series of referentialist grunts. Just as dining can never be explained by eating or loving solely by sex, the primitive origins are inadequate to explain, just because, *as* primitive, such origins are purposive. This is Glaucon's protest in the *Republic:* one cannot achieve a true understanding of the state merely by reference to mutual assistance for the sake of the satisfaction of citizens' basic wants and needs. So just as Plato is required to understand the ordinary state by reference to the ideal one, so our attempt to understand language must appeal not to its ordinary, possibly communicative, uses but to its extraordinary achievement in poetry or other lofty instances, such as oratory, philosophical disputation, and the prayers of worship.

As was noted earlier, one does not first desire to dwell and then hire an architect to accomodate this desire; rather dwelling as such becomes possible for the first time only through architecture. So, just as an architect, by his art, changes a mere place of protection from the elements (which is purposive) to a place of dwelling (which is existential), and thereby reveals or unfolds *what it means to dwell at all,* so poetry, by transcending the mere communicative use of language, reveals existentially what it means to have truth at all. Dwelling, as revealed in architecture, is a dimension of who we are, insofar as it unfolds the meaning of having a home or place where we belong; so poetry reveals language as unfolding truth.

We can return to the image of the primitive user of sounds to designate things and to express his basic needs. If these prelinguistic grunts are sufficient, then why should he ever speak at all? He need not speak to discover the cave where he crawls for protection, nor to satisfy his hunger by wolfing down the berries and game; he need not speak to satisfy the puzzling carnal instincts within him when he spies a female, nor need he speak to explain or justify his acts, since he simply does what he must. Why then would he speak? Perhaps to worship. Or to thank. Or to wonder. He must speak, and not merely communicate, if he is to make sense of who he is, if he is to tell the early stories of how he came to be; he must speak if he is to matter. But this is language, not communication, and so it takes the form of stories and poems and prayers, and just as his neighbor, the builder, changes everything by revealing dwelling in his architecture, so the speaker changes everything by revealing truth in his language. Thus, language lets truth unfold. It is not "this" sentence or "that" sentence which makes a world appear, and thereby allows for the unfolding of truth, but simply speaking in general. Language as an existential possibility is more fundamental than particular uses of language. Nor should we focus our attention solely on the sentences which we happen to know are true—which would be a dreadful instance of *petitio principii* —nor only on proper and correct analyses of essences; for the poet does not say that "a *true* sentence uttered makes a world appear," since the world allows for both honesty and deception. Language with its lies, its cleverness, its enchantment, its deception, its majesty, and its profanation; language with its power to raise the heart and mind to giddy heights, and to dash it whimpering in pornographic baseness; language as praying and cursing, as cruel and tender; language that pardons and language that intones the fell doom of a death sentence, or the denial of love; language as sarcastic and ironic, tawdry and playful; language as magnificently ambiguous and as bitter blasphemy—only in its fullest range can language make a world appear, for a world is a big place, a dwelling of saints and sinners, and if it is to be brought out into appearance by a sentence, the sentence must be rooted in language as broadly conceived as the cunning of speech will allow. For even in its darkest intonations— cursing, lying, profaning, insulting, swearing, punning, making false oaths, libeling, and defiling—a sentence *still* makes a world appear, and only *when* a world appears can there be truth. There is no violation of the prohibition against contradiction here, as if we were to say that all lies are true. Rather, in telling a lie we display language, and in this display of language a world appears, and only if the world appears can there be truth. It is, of course, the truth which allows us to recognize the lie, but it is the lie as language which, in making a world *appear*, lets truth unfold. It is in language as the source that lets a world appear that the very distinction between lying and truth can first be made.

Those who worship language revere not merely the success of language, such as true sentences or honorable promises, but perhaps even more the beguiling arts, the lies and curses and forswearings, for here the power of language is revealed autonomously, and not merely as a vehicular servant of knowledge.

To render a sufficient account of this rich notion is fortunately neither necessary nor possible in this brief analysis, for the primary concern here is not with language itself or even with *how* language can make a world appear and hence provide for the unfolding of truth. It is enough for the present inquiry merely to suggest *that* this is true and to sketch out enough to show what it means. Hopefully these brief reflections have shown that language is not a mere freighter bearing the commerce from one port to another, but rather that which makes visible the entire pounding and heaving sea which washes all shores. It is, as Heidegger says, "the house of Being"; which means that, unlike furniture which can be brought in or thrown out, it encloses and provides a place for existence to matter. Something like Heidegger's metaphor or Auden's stanza must be assumed if truth unfolds as a story.

We tell a story with language, but not as an instrument, the way we use the telephone to communicate. Rather, language makes a world appear, and in so doing reveals the storylike power of truth to reveal. One final consideration as to the storylike (that is, historical) nature of truth remains.

Truth and Time

If truth unfolds through language, and if the world, conceived either as reality or as actuality, appears in the telling of a story, then the unfolding nature of time itself must be assumed. There is something misleading about the locution "in time," as if time were a receptacle, greater even than the world itself—for we speak of the world being "in time"—and as if whatever is in time, whether it be the world or life or truth or language, could somehow exist "outside of time." The phrase brings to mind the image of time as a moving train onto which we can jump and ride along for a while, but from which we could—or at least would like to be able to—jump off. But of course, such an image is distortive and misleading. Whatever else time is, it is not an arbitrary characteristic that can be assigned as a nonnecessary predicate to notions. On the other hand, the inevitability of time is often used as an argument against anything absolute or universal: because reality is temporal, it is argued, so too must truth be temporal, and this means truth is changing, epoch-determined, and relative to the changing perspectives of growth. This argument is invalid, for it confuses different times with time itself, and the unfolding of truth with the disparity between frozen frames of temporal units. Indeed it is only because both the world and its unfolding in truth are temporal that there exists even the possibility of an absolute or of universals. To characterize truth as essentially temporal is not to make it relative but simply to make it interesting. (One might ask: relative to what? If one responds, relative *to* the specific epoch or moment *in* time, the deep error is exposed; for time is not derived from discrete moments, rather moments are abstractions from the reality of time. If one responds by saying that truth is relative to time itself, then truth is not relative in the ordinary sense, but absolute, for 'time itself' is not 'in time'.)

But time should not be given some supermetaphysical status like the medieval notion of God. Time, like other broad notions such as 'world' and 'truth', is perhaps not so much mysterious and distant as overly familiar and ubiquitous—indeed, 'the constancy of time' sounds oxymoronic and vaguely humorous. Happily this inquiry does not require us to provide a complete metaphysical description of time; we need only show how time belongs in the understanding of truth as a story, or of truth as historical.

The famous Aristotelian analysis of dramas as requiring a beginning, a middle, and an end suggests that this tripartite division is *essential*, and thereby *necessary*, to understand the unfolding of a story. There is a corresponding tripartite division in reality itself, or rather, to be more precise, in our being in the world—the division into past, present, and future. Just as the events in a story are meaningful only because of the story, and not the other way around, so the notion of our being in the world in terms of our past, present, and future makes our events meaningful, and not the other way around. In both cases, the story or the history is more fundamental. The individual events, by themselves, are meaningless; it is only because they belong to a broader understanding of the interrelatedness (the story) of these occurrences that we can think about them—that is, that they are meaningful. (For "to be meaningful" just means "to be thinkable in some way.")

In a story, we think about the beginning as pregnant with the impending meaning to be unfolded, as is evidenced in the opening line of "The Princess and the Pea." The middle dramatizes by linking the opening with the conclusion, and the end shows us the thinkability of the earlier events in the light of the resolution. But if truth has the form of a story, then this same structure of intelligibility should apply to the phases of time itself. By the term 'past' we mean that which is pregnant with what will unfold as meaningful only in terms of subsequent development; by the present we mean the unfolding of this meaning; and by the future we mean the meaning as unfolded or revealed. Our existence is in time, which means it is unfolded in the telling of the story which makes it meaningful, and this results in the realization that the past, present, and future are not dislocated, isolated instances but elements of the greater unfolding power of truth.

In no way is this analysis intended to suggest a metaphysics of process; nor does it deny permanence or infinity or even a necessary being— indeed no metaphysical claims are intended at all. Rather, the analysis focuses solely on how one must understand time if truth is to be storylike or historical, that is, if truth unfolds. The idea that truth has a storylike form—that it unfolds as a story—is not without precedent. Indeed, the storylike nature of truth can be seen in terms of certain classically important notions. If events are not meaningful except as they occur in a context or a story, then as things develop toward a resolution, the way an acorn develops toward a towering oak, it would seem that their terminus is the source of their intelligibility. Accordingly, Aristotle argues that a child *becomes,* whereas a man *is,* and that the man is hence the *telos* or purposive source of intelligibility of the growing or becoming child. If one starts with an event or object in the present and works backwards, one finds what are called efficient causes; if one works forward, one finds final or purposive causes. Thus, the present frost on my windshield was caused by last night's subfreezing temperature, whereas my scraping this frosted pane is for the future purpose of being able to drive prudently with sufficient vision. The past caused what is present, the future explains what I presently do. Such explanations are surely correct, and without the notion of a purpose, which usually looms in the future, I simply cannot make sense of much of what happens. We might appeal once more to our earlier distinction and say that purpose gives us what is *true* about the future. But it does not produce an understanding of time as being in *truth*.

To understand the temporal character of truth as unfolding, it is insufficient to appeal to cause (past) and purpose (future). Rather, we must appeal to another notion of the Greeks, found in the way they tell their stories: they begin *in medias res*. The *Iliad* begins right in the middle of the Trojan War; *Antigone* opens with Polyneices already dead and Creon's laws already promulgated; *Oedipus* begins with the hero already guilty of incest and patricide. One tells the story by letting the *past* become as threatening and menacing as the *future*. The suspense is not only in what *will* happen but in what *has* happened. This approach to the great art forms of the epic and tragic tellings suggests that perhaps it is not only or exclusively *purpose* which makes the future intelligible, but tragic or comic inevitability.

How is it possible to *think* about the future and the past? Not as causes, whether efficient or final, but as elements revealed in the telling of the story. In other words, neither the future nor the past—nor even the present—is intelligible at all *except* insofar as they presuppose each other. Many outrageous claims about time arise from the simple error of conceiving time as a construct of more fundamental units; but any worthwhile account of time recognizes that the past, present, and future are derived from time rather than the other way around. It is even more misleading to focus on the metaphysical character of this tripartite division, for when pressed none of the three can be independently existent. The past obviously does not exist, since it is no longer, and the future does not exist because it is not yet. This might seem to isolate the present as independently existent, but a moment's reflection shows that the present, sheered of all that is past and all that is future, is so knife-edged that it, too, vanishes into nothingness like Zeno's ultimate particle. Obviously, then, it is not the past, present, or future that exists, but time itself. Even so it is difficult to imagine how time itself, containing all three tenses, could be said to *exist*. Rather, just as truth unfolds the world as reality (or actuality), so time unfolds being. Language, when uttered, makes the world appear, and in its appearance truth unfolds as a story unfolds; so time unfolds the meaning of being: thus there is an isomorphism between the tripartite division of a story into a beginning, a middle, and an end, and the tripartite division of being unfolding as past, present, and future.

The technique of beginning a story *in medias res* reveals that the present (middle) is meaningful (dramatic) just because of what is revealed as preceding the drama in the past (beginning) and what transpires as the tragic or comic inevitability in the looming future (end). The end is not, however, as Aristotle sees it, a purposive end, but simply an end in the sense of dramatic inevitability. Thus in its existential meaning dramatic inevitability, though in no way predictable, and hence unsuitable for *knowledge,* provides the story with its truth in exactly the same way that time, as the unfolding of being, provides the thinker with truth as historical. To be in truth is to be revealed by the unfolding of time.

This argument deserves reiteration and analysis. The first point is the fairly obvious one that time is more fundamental than the moments into which we divide it. A thousand bricks may make up a wall, in which case the wall is a construct of the fundamental elements, the bricks. But this is disanalogous to time. As early as Zeno it was seen that time is not a construct of divisible moments. But it is not only the smallest divisions of time that cannot construct time; the tenses past, present, and future are not independent in any way whatsoever. The intelligibility of time requires that we conceive of the three tenses in terms of principles which unify them. So the question arises: how are the three tenses of time thought as a unity?

An attractive possibility has occurred to some very wise men, led by the genius of Aristotle—namely, that the interrelation of the tenses is grounded in principles of explanation. Imagine standing before a magnificent seventeenth-century hall, built chiefly of wood, standing in a grove of oak trees. We pick up an acorn, and look at the mighty oak that spreads out before us. That tree was once a mere acorn. Going back into time we can imagine the original acorn as the dominant cause of the present tree. This connects the present oak with the previous acorn by the principle of efficient causality. But this oak can be felled by woodsmen and made into boards by lumbermen and built into a hall by carpenters. We think of the presently confronted oak as having a purpose: to provide us with the stuff with which to build the hall. This connects the present oak with the future building by means of a final cause or a purpose. The present display of the spreading branches provides us with the form of the tree, and the constancy of the woodlike elements from acorn to tree to building provides us with the notion of material. Hence Aristotle's four great causes—efficient, formal, material, and final—can be seen not only as linking the acorn to the oak, and the oak to the building, via the constancy of the material; but also as linking the past (acorn), the present (tree), and the future (building), and providing the notion of persistence obtaining through the changes (the wood). Thus the past, the present, the future, and the linkage of time itself are accounted for by these fundamental principles of explanation, usually translated "causes" with considerable loss of the original Greek meaning.

There is no doubt that these four ways of explaining events do indeed provide a notion of interrelated tenses which allows us to think of time as a unity of events. Indeed, in this respect it is easy to understand why Aristotle gave special status to the purposive or final cause—not because it merely ends the series, but because it provides the compelling link from one stage to another. Because I can see the acorn in my hand as ultimately providing the beams with which the hall is constructed, the greater reality, the hall, has more illuminative value than the humble beginning, the acorn.

But is this the only way to link the three tenses of time? And even if it is *one* way, is it philosophically the best? We have another model, the dramatic unfolding of a story, which has not only a beginning, a middle, and an end, but also characters, plot, and theme. In the unfolding of the story the interconnection of past, present, and future is not incidental, as it seems in the process from the acorn to the hall, but dramatically inevitable. We *understand* the past as that which, like a womb sired by implantation, gives us *character;* we *understand* the present as the giving birth in the dramatic unfolding of *plot;* and we *understand* the future as the tragic or comic resolution, that is, the death or the new implanting by the reconciled young lovers, in the *theme.* The unifying principle is here the story itself.

These two accounts are both valuable; they both unify the variant tenses and hence make time meaningful. The first gives us knowledge, the second gives us truth. But truth is nobler than knowledge, and the story more illuminating than causal explanations. In any event, the temporal character of our existence corresponds to the unfolding character of language as it reveals truth. In this way our understanding of world as historical helps us with our assigned task, the nature of truth as unfolding.

11

The World as Home and Tribunal

The World as Home

The world is our home; we belong
in it. In order to comprehend truth as the unfolding of the world, it is
necessary to grasp that the world is neither a place (for a place
presupposes the world) nor an entity (for an entity is always *within* the
world) but rather the necessary condition for being able to dwell at all.
To say the world is our home may strike some readers as simply
romantic nonsense, for homes, like places, are always somewhere in the
world, which is precisely what the world cannot be. Furthermore the
notion that the world is our home seems to give the purely emotive term
'home' an entirely inappropriate metaphysical status. Homes, one may
object, are simply places within the world to which we attach a certain
fondness or affection, and since the world contains all such places it is
meaningless to suggest that the world is our home.

These objections are not without merit; but they are not fatal. In
spite of them, it will be shown that the world *is* our home and that
we *do* belong here. However, the analysis requires that the meanings
of certain terms be deeply penetrated and examined in the light of
the central theme, truth. As has been shown, truth unfolds the reality
of the world, so that the world itself must be seen as a home as well
as a story. Thus we must first ask: what is meant by 'home'? Since many
ideas reveal their meanings when contrasted with their opposites, one
possible route of inquiry would be to consider the two modes of existence which reveal what it means to be *without* a home: exile and
homesickness.

Exile.   In the first act of Shakespeare's *Richard II*, the king inter-
rupts the duel between Bolingbroke and Mowbry:

> For that our kingdom's earth should not be soiled
> With that dear blood which it hath fostered;
> And for our eyes do hate the dire aspect
> Of civil wounds plough'd up with neighbor's sword;
> . . . .
> Therefore we banish you our territories.
>
> (I.3)

To which Mowbry replies:

> What is thy sentence then but speechless death
> Which robs my tongue from breathing nature's breath?
> . . . .
> Then thus I turn me from my country's light
> To dwell in solemn shades of endless night.
>
> (I.3)

For Mowbry to be banished is a fate no less grim than death itself, particularly because without his native English, he will no longer be able to speak. Banishment in the Elizabethan age was a dread punishment, since it deprived the exile of all that was his own. The loss of English is made all the more onerous for us, the audience, since as we witness this play we hear our tongue in its most radiant and exquisite form. Perhaps only *Romeo and Juliet* can equal the poetic loveliness of this tragedy of the second Richard. Indeed, in the love-tragedy, Romeo too is exiled by the Prince, whose edict is passed on to the sequestered Montague by Friar Laurence:

> FRIAR: A gentler judgment vanish'd from his lips,
>   Not body's death, but body's banishment.
> ROMEO: Ha! Banishment! Be merciful, say 'death';
>   For exile has more terror in his look
>   Much more than death, do not say banishment.
>
> (III.3)

It is not necessary to explore in detail why these two characters from Shakespeare lament their enforced exile. Home is where one not only learns but shares the exquisite delights of language, custom, religion, family, and protection. However, these Shakespearean passages merely give us some hint as to what the Elizabethan mind thought about exile. Even if we grant these insights as revealing of another age, what has this to do with us? Modern jets and international telephones and television, together with a less parochial sense of belonging only in one place, all conspire to deny the immediate sense of loss felt by Mowbry and Romeo. Scarcely anyone today regards exile as worse than death. Nevertheless, these quotations from the Elizabethan age give us a hint of what it means to be deprived of one's home, and from this negative beginning we may be able to isolate what 'being at home' means, and with this understanding apply it to the world.

The key to this comprehension is the recognition that exile deprives us of meaning, or at least makes meaning more difficult to achieve. In exile we are banished from what is our own, and from where we belong. This alone shows us what is meant when we describe the *world* as our home. To be exiled from the world is parallel to being exiled from our native land.

But the world contains all local places, including Verona and England; indeed if exile means being driven away from home, then an exile from the world is entirely incoherent. How can we be banished from the *world?* There are those, of course, who remove themselves from the familiar and social world and seek out isolation, either to achieve the anchorites' privative communication with the divine, or simply because they have found the world so repugnant and corrupt that they take leave of it. Timon of Athens is a good example of this self-imposed exile from the 'world' of people and society. Although Timon is still *in* the world, he is estranged from it by his contempt. His exile is not merely from Athens but from all human intercourse, and so it is possible to see Timon as an exile from the world.

But such hatred and contempt is fairly rare, and may perhaps always be a form of mental dementia and hence of little worth for a philosophical inquiry. However, one need not be a recluse or an anchorite to be an exile from the world who remains in the world. The difference is between those who merely exist *in* the world and those who *dwell* in the world. As we have just seen, exile is considered a torment because one is cut off from one's origins and culture and from where one belongs. But one can act and think in such a way as to make 'belonging' an entirely irrelevant characteristic. Unlike the antisocial Timon, someone who rejects belonging to the world may continue to interact socially with others and even succeed in everyday enterprises. But he is in exile all the same, alienated from what is his own by the very conscious decision not to belong at all, anywhere. Such an exile consists in the existential denial of all belonging, and since such denials are made often enough, and by sane and coherent nonhaters, their reasoning must be closely examined.

Why should anyone deliberately banish himself from the world? The answer is freedom—or, to be more precise, a kind of false freedom which entails a denial that one belongs anywhere whatsoever. The argument is sound enough: as long as I have a home, or belong somewhere, by the bonds of blood or the accidents of birth, I am, to that extent, unfree. Freedom in this sense is a conscious and deliberate option, in which one considers the appeals of both belonging and freedom, and chooses the latter. He who opts for this 'freedom' considers the advantages to himself sufficient to close off any sense of duty, responsibility, reverence for tradition, or ties of blood. It is a way of thinking and of being which, unlike the misanthropy of Timon, ranks the unfettered and untroubled existence of the radically free individual above that of one who belongs to the world. Since such a one may find pleasure and even happiness in the society of others, he has no inclination to misanthropy except in that rare and unusual sense of refusing to admit to any duties or obligations. Just as it is possible for there to be a "man without a country," so too, in this special sense, can there be a "man without a world."

Enforced exile in the parochial sense, as endured by Mowbry and Bolingbroke, is intelligible to us because the banishment severs one perforce from one's home. Self-induced exile from the world is the adoption of a radically free and hence ultimately homeless existence. To such an exile the prospect of losing his home or culture is no threat, since he freely opts for this kind of alienation by ranking his own autonomy as a boon superior to any kind of sharing or togetherness which he has not himself chosen merely for his own delight. The anchorite in the desert seeks to disjoin his existence from others, but the exile from the world believes that the only meaningful existence is one in which he alone chooses or selects those with whom he wishes to consort.

Freedom is a precious commodity, but so too is meaning. Truth can occur only to one who belongs to the world, not to one who merely resides in it. This is in no way meant to imply that outgoing, garrulous, and overly friendly types are more meaningful than lonely, isolated, and reclusive types. Indeed, the exile in question is usually quite social, perhaps even noisy, glad-handing, back-slapping, and even pestiferous. What distinguishes him is his peculiar way of thinking which isolates or maroons him on the tiny atoll of inauthentic freedom. In this way it is possible to achieve an exile from the world even as we continue to live in it.

But the parochial sense of exile enforced on Romeo and Mowbry was seen as a kind of punishment. The exile from the world is likewise punished—though solely on his own initiative—but he is unaware of the cost. Being in the world but not dwelling in it provides him with an unconscious loneliness, making the entire world alien. Like all exiles he is cut off from what is his own, but he is blinded by the false light of radical autonomy. It is not necessary to depict this unfortunate exile in detail; the sketch is made solely for the purpose of isolating what it means to belong to the world by showing how it is possible *not* to belong to the world.

Homesickness.

> Look homeward Angel, now, and melt with ruth,
> And, O, ye dolphins waft the helpless youth.
>
> Milton, "Lycidas"

Banishment, or exile, is an active alienation from what is one's own, but homesickness is a passive endurance which the victim suffers just because he *has* a home, and longs for it. It is easy enough to imagine, or remember, what it is like. And although its more acute form is usually found among children who suddenly find themselves aching to return home, homesickness can also disrupt the life of an adult or even an entire people. In all of its forms, however, it manifests an unusual realization that we are people with a *place*, that '*who* we are' is determined in part by 'where we belong'. That such a recognition should occur at all is surprising, especially in our present antihome culture, where individuality is seemingly regarded as the highest virtue. Homesickness need not always be for a remembered place; for many it is a vague, flickering hope for something available only in the future, like the "promised land, flowing with milk and honey" that the Hebrews longed for. Or one can be homesick for a place one has not yet identified, hoping that the future will provide one with a home.

Most cases of homesickness are accompanied by an unusual and therefore unexpected discovery about ourselves: we are, to some degree, characterized by where we dwell. If the previous chapter reveals the importance of time, this chapter reveals the importance of place. The homesick suffer an unusual agony, for it is nothing less than the appeal to who we are. We realize that our wants and desires are not alone as possible promptings for action, that we must acknowledge our sense of belonging. That homesickness is possible at all is a remarkable revelation, for without this curious ache to return or to arrive eventually *at* a place that is ours, we would not be able to understand the more general notion that the world is our home.

But parochial homesickness is a specific and nonuniversal sentiment, important perhaps in widening the sense of who we are. How, then, is it possible to ache for the world? As in the case of the exile, is not the victim of homesickness merely a local or political phenomenon? It seems that one cannot be homesick for the world, but only for specific places within the world.

To be able to "look homeward," as Milton bids his angel to do, and see in that 'home' the world itself, is possible only if by the term 'world' we mean a bestowal of sheltering welcome, a formal condition for belonging at all. In other words, homesickness for the world is impossible if the world is a metaphysical abstraction or even an abstract entity. The world is rather the womb of meaning, the anchorage which provides the wind-tossed ship a solid place to link up with some security. It is a hearth from which we inherit the warmth that makes things matter.

The exile is one who, desirous of freedom, seeks to escape from this anchorage and enjoy the wanton and wayward dance from wave to wave; but the homesick, unlike the exile, has not *opted* for such dubious freedom, but because of bad thinking is unable to find the spot where his ship's anchor can find solidity. The exile's error is of the will, the homesick errs in his mind, for he misprizes or simply misunderstands what the world is. To be able to be homesick for the world requires that the world be familiar to us as a source of comfort, warmth, meaning, and ultimately truth. As the conceptual and cognitive establish firmer strangleholds on our thinking, particularly in the academic and entertainment industries, more and more ideas become abstract. When the world itself achieves the status of abstraction, we lose any intimacy with it, and all things become alien. Logicians and literary critics alike speak of possible worlds, and in so doing create an atmosphere of total alienation, where kinship (the opposite of alienation) becomes impossible.

Only if the world is our home can existence be adventurous, and only in this kinship of the world can truth be unfolded. For if there are possible worlds, or only perspectives or representations, and hence no reality anywhere to latch onto, not only truth but authentic freedom itself is impossible. The world is our home and we belong in it. But what does this last phrase mean?

Belonging. We belong in the world, first because as historical it grounds the genealogy of truth, and second because, as home, it grounds what is our own as truth. We have found, then, both a time and a place in the world. We can therefore now examine the fundamental notion of the world as home: belonging.

The verb 'belong' has a curious imperative—almost moral—sense to it. If we say "she belongs on the stage" we seem to suggest there is something compelling or proper about where she should be. This is, of course, a nonmoral imperative, for in saying "she belongs on the stage" we do not mean to say she would be immoral if she were not to become an actress. Even when we seem to equate "this is my home" with "I belong here," there is no moral sense that I *ought* to remain in my home. 'Belonging' can designate possession, as when we equate "this belongs to me" with "this is mine: I *own* it." But 'belonging' also seems to imply a sense of self-realization, so that belonging seems to *complete* what in its absence would leave us unfinished or out of place.

What does it mean, then, to 'belong to the world'? As a philosophical notion it means that any attempt to make sense of me which leaves out how I am in the world is misguided. The world is not "out there," as if, in some way, we could imagine a knowing mind not in the world. Furthermore, it means that the world is not the sum total of all entities, nor is it the entity large enough to contain all others. For consider this analysis: "I do not have any empirical knowledge of the world, only of entities within the world." The sentence seems obviously true, but the consequences of its truth are remarkable. If I cannot know the world by experience, then either the world does not exist at all, or the term 'world' has no meaning at all (in spite of the last four words of the sentence), or it designates a Kantian-type category which is supplied by the mind to provide a sense of continuity and unity among entities. But all three of these suggestions are highly dubious. To equate the world with the sum total of all entities is merely to abstract the notion to its highest level and to admit that the term adds nothing to any knowledge claim.

For the world to have a meaning other than that of a purely conceptualized receptacle containing all entities it must be approached from an existential rather than an epistemological standpoint. The world is not so much known as it is recognized; that is, it does not come into my view the way a bus appears from around the curve in the street, nor is it a category, like causality, through which I filter my various experiences and hence understand them. Rather, from its first inception as an idea, the world is already familiar as that which establishes the possibility of being true, as where we belong. To belong in the world is to say that (1) we are not alone, that is, we are not isolated knowing subjects, but sharers and fellow members of a vast community, and (2) existential truth or meaning is grounded in a nonarbitrary way.

What do we mean, for example, when we say that one belongs to a social club? As a member of the club I have joined with others for some purpose or project. Together, the members are more than they are merely as individuals; what binds them together is their sharing of interests and willingness to accompany the others. The purpose is either trivial, as a bridge club, or annoying, as a political party, or professional, as an academic society. In all of these examples, the sense of belonging is established on the basis of some common interest or need. How then can we "join" the world-club? What is it that accounts for our gathering together in the society known as the world? The answer is truth. For only if we *belong* to the world is it possible for truth to matter. We have seen that one sense of 'belonging' is to make something our own. (This is my *own* book means: this book *belongs* to me.) The world is our own. In a cosmic homesickness I can become lost by thinking badly, or I can exile myself in order to free myself from the burden of belonging, but in both cases what is *meant* by the world from which I am estranged is precisely that mode of existence which I *should* (though not in the sense of moral compulsion) recognize as belonging. I belong in the world, and the world belongs to me—for without "world," neither "I" nor "me" would be possible.

Just as a family is necessary in order for there to be a brother or a sister, an uncle or a grandmother, so the world is necessary for there to be what is my own—even for me to use the first-person pronouns. It is because I *dwell* in the world *as* my own that truth can unfold. The world is the anchor of all meaning, and unless I am a *part* of it, and not merely an *onlooker*, meanings become unanchored, and hence meaningless.

What are the philosophical consequences of recognizing the world as a home in which to dwell? There are three results which cannot be overestimated. (1) The world is now seen as the ground not only of factual claims, but of values and issues of human significance. If the world is my home, I must care about it and regard it as the depository of weighty matters. No longer can I separate the 'external world' of value-less events from an 'internal world' where the caring subject invests its interests. (2) With the world as my own, it is now possible, indeed essential, to establish in the world the determination of what is my own, so that making things my own is now a part of truth. And (3) it is possible to be in the world but not dwell in it, and thereby to succeed or fail; or, in other words, just *because* the world is historical *and* is my home, it also becomes a tribunal.

All three of these consequences are important for their own sake, but even more than that, they undermine the essentially nihilistic view that divides judgments into 'subjective' and 'objective'. There is no longer any sound basis for an isolated and unanchored subject or an external and radically other object. The world is both, for it contains the subject and reveals the object. This does not quarantine the distinction altogether; it merely denies metaphysical or ultimate status to objects and subjects. But, most important, it permits us to see the *world* as the ultimate tribunal of worth.

The World as Tribunal

To exist is to be judged. Strictly speaking, of course, the sentence should read "to exist as a conscious being is to be able to be judged," but since the more accurate description is less elegant, we can assume these refinements and continue to acknowledge the truth of the sentence. But if "to exist is to be judged," then one must ask: by what authority? or before what tribunal? The answer to both questions is the world. The world is the ultimate tribunal of all judgments. If there are any lesser tribunals—as there obviously are, from legal courtrooms to parental anger, or even to a professor reading examination books—it is always possible to remove oneself from those arenas of censure and simply go elsewhere. But some judgments transcend these local tribunals, and appear to have universal validity—that is, the validity of the universe, the world. Thus I may escape the tribunal of a harsh state which would imprison me for my acts by simply migrating to a more lenient state where my acts are either permitted or only mildly censured. A prudent killer may select a state without capital punishment lest he be apprehended and have to face the sanction. But the judgment that it is immoral to murder is independent of the statutes which have rendered murder illegal. I need a state to declare an act illegal; I need a world to ground the judgment that the person is immoral.

But how can this be? Surely judgments of success or failure are found not in the world but merely in personal agents who are within the world. Indeed, one of the advantages of the world is its amoral neutrality. It rains upon the just and the unjust, and only thinking beings can succeed or fail. Furthermore, if the world is a tribunal, subpoenas should be available in nature, which is absurd. It is impossible to find little nuggets of guilt or innocence lying in the creek bed like gold or pyrite. These reflections make it entirely unlikely that the preceding paragraph is true.

The world should never be equated with nature. Obviously one cannot find nuggets of guilt as one finds nuggets of gold, but that is merely because the world is more than nature. Furthermore, if we protest that thinking subjects somehow make judgments solely on their own authority, such subjects are in the world, and hence the world contains them, so that all judgments are still in and of the world. However, the claim that the world is our tribunal does not mean merely that judging creatures, like men living together under manmade laws, are a part of the world. Rather, to say the world is our tribunal is to acknowledge the world as the source of all judgments, and not merely a part of the world (the human part), leaving nature amoral and neutral. What then, does it mean to say the world is our tribunal?

The first and obvious point is that, if the world is our tribunal, we can no longer rely on subjectivist escapes to avoid the burden of our thinking. The world as tribunal is what makes such judgments not merely valid or coherent, but true. And this is a terribly important discovery, for now it can be argued that "Thou shalt not lie" is not merely a parochial or provincial belief, but something that can be true or false. The study of nature will never yield a single 'ought' (as we learn from Hume, 'is' does not imply 'ought'), but the study of the *world* certainly will. For by the term 'world' is meant the ultimate resource for all that is intelligible, from facts and events to meanings and commands. The world is not merely the physical world but also the moral and aesthetic world. It is neither the sum total of all physical entities (nature) nor some ideal spawned by the creative powers of the mind. As we have seen earlier, the world is both actuality and reality, and truth is the unfolding of the world in both senses.

Never has the seductive power of Enlightenment thinking been more persuasive, nor more beguiling, than in this all too convenient division of the world from matters of worth and value. Ever since Descartes, the metaphysical disjunction of the mind from the world and the world from the mind has fettered our thinking and freighted it with so profound an error that even the wisest of men have failed to penetrate beyond these artificial limits. And yet, it is so obviously false that one wonders at its power to persuade as it does. The world is not external to the mind, nor is it to be equated with it. Rather, one must abandon these substantive entities altogether and reflect on what it means to think as a way of being in—or perhaps better, dwelling in—the world. To dwell in the world is to confront moral responsibilities, to submit to the thrall of beauty, to succeed or fail in being who we are, to use particular objects for our purpose, and to recognize, identify, and classify entities within the range of our experience. To dwell in the world *also* is to imagine things that do not exist and to speculate on things that may exist, but the difference between knowing that something is the case and believing that something exists when in fact it does not is not explained by the world/mind distinction. To account for mental images which do not provide knowledge by bringing in the heavy artillery of metaphysics is dangerous strategy. Distinctions, of course, must be made: a statement of fact is not a value judgment. But such distinctions do not have the awesome metaphysical power of dualism. Nor do they support any kind of reductionism, either to matter or to mind; for the simple truth is that the world is quite vast enough to contain both without becoming either. To say that truth unfolds reality—and hence the world—is to recognize that insofar as judgmental assertions belong to what is unfolded—the world—truth also reveals our success and our failure. Success and failure are in and of the world; they are not merely 'mental states', much less illusions or emotions. And because the world is both our home and our history, its unfolding in truth is also our tribunal. We have seen that to be is to be historical, and that to be is to belong. We now add: to be is to be judged. In all three cases what anchors our story, our home, or our mattering is the world. But 'judgment' here does not necessarily imply praise or censure; rather it merely means that assessments of the worth of things, actions, people, and ways of existence are *possible*. What makes them possible is the world.

It is, of course, an oddity born of introverted speculation that would limit the meaning of the world to mere factual events and entities. Such a limitation, necessary for technological manipulation or even some kinds of science, is absurd when applied to the world in its entirety. The world is more than particles and fields of energy; it is also our hates and loves, our forgiveness and wonder, our history, our destiny, and our guilt. I do not say the world is the *place* in which all these things happen; I say the world *is* our hating, loving, and doubting, along with the atoms and particles that make up our forks and whips and mirrors; the world is even our mystery. It is, because of this, our home; and because one of the ways we *think* is to judge, rank, censure, blame, and assess, the world is the ultimate tribunal.

We judge, of course, in different ways. We condemn evil and praise goodness, we reject the ugly and affirm the lovely, we admire the virtues and envy the vices even as we debase them. But most of all we confront the tribunal, the world, in terms of our own worth. Are we who we ought to be? Are we true to ourselves? Such questions are not about unworldly, foreign subjects, but about the world and how we fit into it. To disjoin both morality and existential authenticity from the world is impossible, though almost all contemporary value theorists do so. This is due, in part, to the Cartesian inheritance of substantive dualism, but it is also due to a certain form of academic timidity not unlike remaining silent while seeing the emperor naked. For when we consider the matter honestly, what else is this troubling business of judging except the unfolding of the world as reality in truth? That the spirit of modernism insists on the *metaphysical* distinction between fact and value merely intensifies the seriousness of overcoming this nihilistic prejudice.

And such a prejudice is indeed nihilistic. For as soon as one disjoins value from the world it is inevitable that a further disjunction is made between the truth and what matters. Yet, to divorce truth from what matters (fact from value) is a gross disservice to both terms. This point must be stressed: the moral wrongness of promise-breaking is of the *world,* and not of the separated subject merely within the world. Subjects may be *in* the world, but people, in all their sinfulness and glory, *dwell* in the world, thereby making the world a tribunal.

In what way are we to understand the world as a tribunal? Dwelling, rather than merely existing, in the world establishes the world as the ultimate confrontation of our guilt, our innocence, and our forgiveness.

The world, after all, is our origin as well as our final destiny, and because of this we acknowledge the unfolding of the world as truth. For truth alone is the ultimate judge.

To say the world is the ultimate tribunal is not to say that the world is our judge. A tribunal is an institutional condition that makes judging possible, it is not the judge itself. In the legal sense, a courtroom is more than a mere place; it is a creation of laws and procedures for witnesses and evidence, designed and structured to allow a certain kind of activity, the passing of judgment on the force of law, on putative violators of that law. To say that the world is a tribunal is, by analogy, to say that who we are is made intelligible by the assessment of success or failure. In this way, it is not only our *actions* that are assessed, but our very existence. We can succeed or fail at being who we are, and unless there is a tribunal, such success or failure has no meaning.

To recognize the world as tribunal is not to affirm or deny any metaphysical assertions concerning the status of the judge. Even if believers were to insist that God alone judges, the world is still our tribunal; nonbelievers may insist that the judge is a nebulous institution such as a culture or a tradition, but even they must find their tribunal as the world. Inheritors of the Enlightenment may even go so far as to say that *we* alone are judges, but even if we admit such a dubious claim it is still the world that is the tribunal. For the world is, on this understanding, the ultimate guarantor of matters of fact, of assessments of value, of moral censure and blame, even of existential meaning.

The purpose of this analysis is not to consider or even ask *how* we are judged or what kinds of judgments can be made, but simply to show that, if truth is the unfolding of the world, it is not enough merely for the world to be our home and our story, it must also be that which grounds our worth—that is, a tribunal. One further characteristic of the world needs exploration before our analysis of truth as the unfolding of the world as reality can be completed.

12

Beckoning

The blouse or shirt with the top three buttons undone. The door slightly ajar through which discreet mumbling can be heard but not understood. The finely bound book lying open on the desk, the title downward. The hush in the concert hall just before the symphony begins. The sweater that does not quite reach the belt. The unfinished sketch by a master's hand on a discarded page.

These beckon. They provoke because they are incomplete; their allure is in their finitude or their promise. If truth unfolds reality, it does so as a kind of beckoning. Not as a water hole beckons the thirsty traveler, but as an exotic adventure beckons the leisured. For the lure of truth is not a demand we must obey; that is its charm. Truth, unlike knowledge, is never necessary. Yet, neither is it idle or trivial. In beckoning, the world reveals itself as a seducer, while we are revealed as open to enchantment. What enchants us, as the preceding paragraph suggests, is precisely what is beyond knowledge or beyond our grasp. But if truth is of essences, what is it about essence that entices? And what is the nature of its promise?

Aristotle, in the opening sentence of the *Metaphysics,* asserts that "all men by their nature desire to know"; and he supports this claim by reference to the satisfaction we take in answering our curiosity. But all men by nature do not seek the truth—not even Aristotle would say so—for truth in no way satisfies our curiosity. If we provisionally accept Aristotle's assertion, then the acquisition of knowledge is a natural thing, like slaking our thirst or seeking companionship. The quest for truth, however, is rather *unnatural,* though not perverse. That is, we cannot find in our natures a universal propensity for philosophy, and because of this there must be something about truth which awakens or seduces in the few this extraordinary adventure, the quest for truth. The terms 'adventure' and 'quest' are carefully and deliberately chosen, for the knight's adventures in his noble quest are carried out—if we are to accept the model of courtly love—for the beauty of a woman forever unattainable. If this seeming "romantic" notion of the quest for essences is to make sense, however, we must understand the phenomenon of the world unfolding its truth as a beckoning.

The point can be made by juxtaposition of two terms. If knowledge is power, that is, if knowledge is purposive, and truth is *not* power, since it has no purpose, how are we to understand those who engage in such strenuous labor seeking truth? I may seek to *know* about farming in order to eat and to feed others; but why should I ever seek to wonder about the *essence* of farming? It is surely not the *farmer* who seeks the essence of farming, for only the philosopher or poet raises such unpurposive questions. The farmer *knows* farming, and if his philosophical son fails at grasping or isolating the proper essence, the crops will still grow, the fields will still be ploughed, the harvest will still be reaped. Thus, philosophy, or the quest for truth, is intelligible only if there is a beckoning, a siren call to essential confrontation. If curiosity provokes a will to knowledge in all, what is it that provokes a will to truth in the few?

The first point to be emphasized is that we are indeed beckoned. Philosophers—not merely the professionals with degrees, but all who seek, with wonder, the confrontation of essence—do not freely go about their work, as builders may decide to erect an edifice; rather they are lured into the darkness of the unanswerable. No one chooses philosophy; philosophy chooses those who are vulnerable to its allure. The Greeks called this vulnerability *thauma*, wonder, and those who suffer this affliction are compared with those who suffer the affliction of love, hence the name 'philosopher'. No one who has spent much time in this endeavor can either escape or deny the thrall that lures us down the irretraceable steps. But is this so unusual? Are not musicians similarly enthralled by music, artists by beauty, or the mystic by visions? Perhaps. But in this case the lure is truth, and hence it demands analysis or at least reflection. And the first item of reflection is the blatant fact. Philosophers are not free to be nonphilosophers any more than Caruso was free not to sing or Nijinsky not to dance. Thus, in rendering an account of the lure of truth it is essential to reveal the bonds or chains that enslave. For the claim here is not that *some* thinkers are captives of their thought, for there are some salesmen who are captives of their bargains, some warriors captive of their valor, some seamen captive of the mighty waters. We are not speaking here of the psychological specimen who happens to love his job regardless of what it is; rather we are speaking of an inner compulsion to seek. For it is possible to succeed at an enterprise without being a slave to it, but it is impossible even to conceive of the inquirer without the ligatures that bind him to an endless, though not unmeritorious, quest.

In using the metaphor of seduction or beckoning, it is necessary to point out that in every temptation there are two conflicting forces at work: the lure itself which tempts us beyond ourselves, and the reluctance which would keep us safely within the confines of our own belonging. Far too many thinkers have sought to explicate the beckoning of philosophy solely from the perspective of that which beckons—the truth, apparently. But in such an account we are left without any sense of true beckoning, because they have given us no reason *not* to seek the truth. But any temptation needs to be explained in terms of both the reluctance and the lure. The thirsty wanderer who happens upon a clear waterfall is not *tempted* to drink, for there is nothing to keep him back.

There is a danger in seeking to explicate truth as beckoning, and that is the normal view of temptation as a lure from the good toward the wicked. Truth is not wicked, though its beckoning may seduce us away from what is secure and successful. Nevertheless, there may be something dangerous in the lure of truth, and if this inquiry is to be true to its quest, the beckoning of truth must be seen as a kind of temptation, in which that *from which* one is tempted is a kind of goodness and that *to which* one is beckoned is a kind of danger or enslavement which, if not completely wicked, is at least threatening. However, the purpose of this inquiry is *not* to reveal the emotional or even mental states of the seeker, but to understand truth itself. In rendering a description of truth-seeking as analogous to temptation, it is hoped that much will be learned about truth itself, and not merely how it feels to be lured by the beckoning of truth.

Beckoning is therefore to be seen as a kind of temptation, and temptation must always be interpreted in terms of both the lure and the reluctance. In order to show the philosophical meaning of these two elements, a brief reflection on three classical temptations may be helpful: the *seduction* of Don José by Carmen; the *bargain* with Faust by Mephistopheles; and finally the *beguiling* of Eve by Satan according to Milton.

The three examples are all from literary texts, for reasons that I trust will soon become obvious. Further, these are not merely three *instances* of temptation, they are the paradigms of what is meant by temptation and, hence, beckoning.

Carmen.   On the surface it seems a typical nineteenth-century operatic melodrama. A loyal young soldier rejects his martial duties as well as the girl from back home, and yields to the seduction of a gypsy woman who manages to ensnare him in the criminal antics of a smugglers' band. Bereft of honor, position, and dignity, the youngster is overcome with jealousy when the gypsy falls in love with a bullfighter, and finding she will not return his affection, stabs her outside the bullring. It seems both a sordid plot and emotionally exaggerated, but the music is wonderful and the singing is often pleasant, and so we endure the silliness of the drama, or perhaps overlook it, as we enjoy the musical treat. Of such silly stories are grand operas often made.

But Bizet is the French Wagner. The music is the drama, and under the influence of his genius the story becomes far more tragic than melodramatic, and when both plot and score are seriously studied, the work is revealed as a masterpiece. What is of special significance for this inquiry is the light it throws on the meaning of seduction, which, as has been noted, requires the tension between that which beckons and that which resists. The truly tragic fall of Don José and his beloved Carmen deserves deeper reflection and analysis. The boos and hisses that confronted the opening night's performance were due in part to a misunderstanding of just how great the tragic element is in this opera. It is a remarkable truth that this drama is deserving of the music that reveals it.

It is the character of Don José that makes *Carmen* a truly worthy drama. On the surface it may seem that the lure is simply Carmen's sexual attraction, and the reluctance is his duty to the army; and certainly these elements are present. But José is not merely seduced by Carmen, he sacrifices all that he holds dear for her. Is this momentary blindness caused by lust? Is it deception, based on a false promise? But Carmen does not lie to José or make false promises. She boldly informs him that she is inconstant, but that for the brief period of her passion, it is total. So José is not deceived. (Indeed, neither is Faust or Eve deceived, as we shall see.) Others have been seduced by Carmen before, so why should José's capitulation matter so much? His loyal, even devout nature is such that, once he capitulates, he must honor that surrender with total commitment and forever. He has not merely *lost* his previous honor, he has *sacrificed* it. José does not kill his beloved merely out of jealousy or even out of frustration at having lost all that mattered to him; he kills her because she cannot or will not accept the magnitude of his sacrifice. In the peculiar logic of the demented lover, his dishonor to Micaela and the army can be redeemed only if his present devotion is sacrosanct, and that requires *sacrifice*, not mere *loss*. But Carmen's dismissal of José renders the sacrifice meaningless, and so it usurps the very reason for his passion. It is not that José was blinded about Carmen's real nature, for she is honest about that from the beginning; rather he was blinded about the extent of his own capacity for devotion and sacrifice. (He sacrifices *her* as well as himself in that final and dreadful confrontation.) But sacrifice is something *noble,* whereas disloyalty to what is precious is ignoble. José is disloyal to his soldier's oath and to Micaela, but he understands these losses as *sacrifices,* and hence as ennobling his own rapture for Carmen. He is not so self-deceived as to believe that his violations were morally right; he merely believes that they were consistent with his nature as one who must be loyal. Thus, his yielding to her voluptuousness and her teasing remains morally flawed; but in sinning he has not lost his awareness of himself as forever loyal, and so he must now place his devotion at the feet of the gypsy girl. It is, perhaps, a profane loyalty, but loyalty all the same. It is surely an irrational loyalty, for he *knows* that Carmen cannot remain true to one man. Hence it is sacrificial.

Seduction, therefore, is never the result of mere deception or even of momentary moral venality. In gaining, there is loss. And what one gains is not the mere promised pleasure, but a confrontation of one's own essence. It is the very nobility of Don José that, in seduction, turns on itself, and binds him sacrificially (hence still nobly) to a passion which, in revealing who he is, destroys him. No wonder the first night's audience was unprepared.

Faust.   But audiences are well prepared for the various interpretations of one of the most famous plots in Christian history. The geniuses of Marlowe, Goethe, and Mann have raised this curious and uneven tale to artistic and metaphysical heights. Yet, it remains a puzzling, almost incoherent story of fascinating wisdom. Why should a man of learning surrender his immortal soul for the cheap tricks of magic? Unlike José, Faust is never defeated by the mere voluptuousness of feminine beauty; indeed he seems more delighted by vulgar tricks played on pompous kings and popes. What deserves our focus, however, is not the surface story of a man who sells his soul for a period of magical delight, but the more ingenious question that confronts the tempter Mephistopheles: how does one successfully tempt a great man of lofty spiritual and intellectual powers? And, as an ancillary to this fundamental question, how could a learned and revered man like Faust find all his wisdom and knowledge so dissatisfying? The latter question is answered only banally unless it is supported by an understanding of the former.

Here Goethe's treatment of the story is by far the most fruitful, even though his idealistic-romantic ending itself is a usurpation, cheating us of the deeper rewards of tragedy. (In *this* sense, Marlowe is superior to Goethe.) Like all things Teutonic, Goethe's masterpiece is too *long*, but though its length is a burden to audiences, it does provide us with greater insights into the fundamental question. Let us see the problem from Mephistopheles' point of view. He has been given a truly awesome task, to bring down the soul of a great man. How does one accomplish such a thing? Faust, learned in philosophy, theology, medicine, and law, cannot be defeated by apples or gypsy girls. Indeed, as the play grinds slowly on, it seems as if Mephistopheles will *never* succeed in making Faust so overwhelmed with delight that he will utter the damning phrase: *Verweile doch! Du bist so schön!* Of course, we know the answer: one defeats a great man by his own goodness. And this answer seems almost glib even as it seems true enough. Mephistopheles finally becomes clever enough to endow Faust with the power of *beneficence,* and, so favored, the learned seller of his soul is moved to acknowledge that he is finally satisfied. The resolution dazzles. Does this mean that goodness satisfies more than knowledge? That in goodness we deserve damnation? That such profound wisdom can only be learned from *diabolical* insight? Or is it more subtle: that Faust was tricked by the *pleasure* taken in being good, not in goodness itself? Or is it that beauty outranks both goodness and knowledge? And how could the *German* Goethe treat bargains and promises so lightly? In allowing Faust's soul to be saved because he took *pleasure* in doing good (not merely *doing* good, but *delighting* in it) apparently God is willing to break a contract. Not even Wotan was allowed to do that. The philosophical and theological puzzles heap higher and higher, defying resolution.

But our task is thankfully far more modest. We are concerned solely with the question of seduction, and Mephistopheles' keen insight that only the delight in goodness can tempt a great man. And here we must proceed cautiously. In the original contract, Faust agrees to surrender his soul only when a moment comes whose *beauty* is so overweening that he would make it linger. Thus it is not 'being good' that defeats Faust, but the recognition of the beauty of being good. The beauty of a woman, Gretchen, was not enough to move Faust. Neither was the delight of sheer power and playfulness. Only the beauty of goodness arrested his soul.

Faust is seduced not in the final but in the first act. He is seduced by the very idea of there being so much beauty that even his learned and cynical soul will be captive to it. He does not believe it can happen; that is why he offers his soul so freely. But the possibility, ephemeral as it is, lures so powerfully that he is willing, like Don José, to offer all that is precious for it. Faust has obviously delighted in knowledge, but never to the point of sacrifice, never to the degree of rapture. Only the beauty of goodness, not even goodness itself, can justify such sacrifice. The very beauty of goodness demands sacrifice; but again, if sacrifice is noble, how can it result in the damning of the soul? This is the paradox that Goethe saw, and his resolution is neither romantic nor idealistic but inevitable. To surrender something of great worth without due recompense is, of course, not a noble sacrifice but supreme foolishness. But when the offering is made on behalf of a worthy exchange, the surrender becomes sacrificial. For Goethe's Faust the ultimately beautiful, which he finds only in goodness, is worth the sacrifice of his soul. For Don José, his character as the loyal one makes his capitulation sacrificial. On the other hand, Marlowe's Faust, who sought only pleasure for twenty-four years, did not sacrifice his soul, but simply lost it; this requires that Marlowe characterize Faust as *dubious* of the worth of his soul: he claims he does not believe in it. (Though how could he *not* believe in the immortality of his soul when Mephistopheles, who provides him with the power he wants, assures him the soul *is* immortal? Only if Faust is *self*-deceived. Carmen and Mephistopheles do not *deceive* their victims.)

Eve.   But does not Milton call Satan the great dissembler? Is not Eve deceived? She certainly is *tricked,* for Satan comes to her in disguise, and lies to her about his ability to speak seventeenth-century English. But on the essential matter, that eating of the fruit will bring death, and that to possess the promised knowledge of good and evil will change her, he does not deceive. Indeed, the final tempter of Eve is Eve herself; and the final temptation is based not on false beliefs, but on true ones. This is the greatest of all the temptations, and is accordingly the most enlightening for this inquiry.

What does Milton tell us about the temptation of Eve in Book IX of *Paradise Lost?* To eat of the tree of "knowledge of Good and Evil" has been prohibited by God's decree. Satan, in the guise of a serpent, although telling a few lies, tempts her to eat of the fruit merely by asking questions. Indeed, questions seem to blossom as thickly as the fruit itself. How can Eve be responsible prior to knowing of good and evil? Why deprive this original couple of the only knowledge worth having? If, as Milton assures us, the tree was there to tempt and try them, how could they *be* tempted if they were ignorant of good and evil? And why, Satan asks, is the punishment death? If they are supposed to *obey* God's command, but do so ignorant of its being *good,* how is this meaningful?

Not only Eve but Milton himself seems uncertain as to whether the fatal choice is something to be celebrated or lamented. Furthermore, Adam's decision to eat is based solely on his love for Eve, his not wanting to lose her. What does all this mean?

What Eve achieves, of course, is her autonomy, and hence the possibility of having meaning. Until she herself goes off, leaving Satan alone, and reflects on the meaning of what she is about to do, there is nothing meaningful about her at all. Indeed, it is her own internal reflection, her self-temptation, that provides her with knowledge of good and evil. The actual eating of the fruit is as unnecessary as the love philter in *Tristan und Isolde.* As soon as she *thinks* as she does, critically, she is mortal, and as mortal, she is free.

The theological language of the epic curtails the impact of the problem. God, apparently, created Eve as free. But freedom means precisely what it says—Eve is not free until she completes the act of her creation. Mortals are not created, they are pro-created: Eve finishes the act of creation by *becoming* free. There is rebellion, of course, and disobedience, but they are necessary in order to establish autonomy. Her act was not a conscious violation of her affection for and devotion to God, but simply, on the basis of her reasoning, a sundering of the merely subservient role of total obedience. Slaves obey merely because of the command, but free people obey out of respect that stems from their own autonomy. Without that original realization that she matters on her own—which in itself is to become aware of "the knowledge of good and evil"—Eve could not freely obey at all. Milton's poetry informs us that God had created them to obey freely—which requires Eve to *think* about the implied threat of death and the *will* to make herself (and Adam) matter independently. And so, not only did Eve establish her freedom by rebellion, she also had to provide her own temptation. For the Miltonian text is clear: it is her own internal reasoning that finally prompts her to act. Satan, in a way, is irrelevant; indeed, in the ultimate sense, so too is God.

The loss is Eden, the gain is grace. It is always painful for loving parents to realize that their children no longer depend on them so completely, yet no good parent would have it otherwise. The divine source of Eve must yield to her human achievement. We now must earn our bread by the sweat of our brow and bring forth our children in pain—our pain—but it is now *our* bread and *our* children, and of course that is supremely precious. Perhaps the Miltonian God sighs with relief as Eve completes the act of creation.

This theological and philosophical richness is far beyond the need of the present inquiry, for the story of Eve is important here only as a resource for understanding temptation. The three literary figures Don José, Faust, and Eve provide us with considerable philosophical illumination on the question of seduction, but not our ordinary understanding of temptation, which is strictly moral. If I yield to the temptation to lie in order to avoid unpleasantness, the analysis reveals merely my weakness to do what I ought. It is only because of their *stories* that we can, and must, reflect on the seductions of José, Faust, and Eve. In no way are these reflections capable of lessening our responsibility to resist the baser inclinations of our nature; morally, temptation is nothing else than the struggle between our inclinations and our duty. But as stories, these accounts of seduction reveal far more.

What, then, have these reflections on the nature of seduction revealed? *First,* we learn that seduction, at least in its proper sense, is unintelligible without genuine reluctance, and the source of this reluctance is fundamentally precious. Thus, we must distinguish between mere temptation, which may yield to any lure at all, or one merely strong enough to break the weakest link in our resistance; and true seduction, in which what is in peril is not merely our virtue, and what threatens it is not merely our weakness, but which rather, in imperiling what is precious, reveals that which was hitherto unrecognized as a great value. *Second,* the paradox of seduction is that the worth of that which is lost amplifies with the widening lure of that which is promised, so that both loss and gain become more precious in the tension. *Third,* the one tempted is radically, fundamentally, and implacably altered by the experience. True seduction is almost a metamorphosis, and indeed not always a beneficial one. *Fourth,* what seems to count more than the worth of the promised is the bestowed vulnerability to the lure of the promised. It is not what we received in the seduction, or even *win,* but what we *become;* and what we become is simply fundamentally vulnerable to the beckoning away from what is precious to that which makes us vulnerable — usually beauty of some kind.

And so, if we are to understand truth as a beckoning, how do these elements of seduction reveal what truth means? What is the lure, the sacrifice, the reluctance, and the gain? These questions do not constitute an idle request to fill in the blanks; they belong to the beckoning of truth as intimately as ardor belongs to the seduction of Don José. Indeed, these questions are a part of what is gained in the loss. We must seek to understand the nature of beckoning in truth with the same passion and vulnerability that makes truth possible at all.

We must not yield to the obvious, unless the obvious deserves to be yielded to; hence we do not say that the truth is what lures, as if truth were a form of sexual allure; rather truth is the entire process, containing all the elements. And so it is not truth that lures, but reality, which remains forever partly hidden and partly revealed (like the unbuttoned shirt) in essence. For essence is never just there, naked and available; essence requires work or wooing on the part of the inquirer.

Similarly, we do not say that, in truth, we are beckoned or seduced away from ignorance, which may seem the obvious or unreflective thing to say; for this leaves unexplained why anyone would *want* to be ignorant, and hence leaves the reluctance unexplained. Rather, that which the inquirer is reluctant to surrender in the lure to essential reality is knowledge itself. There is a safety, a security, in the admirable search for knowledge, in which answers terminate as the earned wage of investigation. Knowledge is, as we have seen, beneficial; to yield or surrender this proper and good achievement is no mean sacrifice. Thus, in the lure, there remains forever the *reluctance* to surrender knowledge: this is of the very essence of the phenomenon of truth.

The gain, of course, is similar to that encountered in the three stories, namely, a kind of bestowed vulnerability, a new capacity to ache and hurt. This bestowed vulnerability is wonder, a wonder which can never satisfy or be satisfied. The acceptance of this is the sacrificial element. In becoming vulnerable to the lure of the real, a continuous *sacrificial* submission, constantly countered by a genuine reluctance to yield the satisfaction taken in knowledge, must be sustained. This lure (essential reality) resists the pull of the reluctance to it (the satisfaction in knowledge), creating a willingness to sacrifice (the ache so essential for inquiry), and the sacrificer gains a new vulnerability (wonder). Thus analyzed, the entire phenomenon of lure, reluctance, sacrifice, and vulnerability is revealed as truth.

We remarked above, however, that in seduction the seduced is radically changed. What is this change in the inquirer's yielding to the seduction of truth? How are we forever different? The change is simply that truth now matters, perhaps ultimately. This does not sound like a great discovery, but in light of the foregoing it most certainly is. Beyond this, however, no mere analysis can reveal—the change must be endured. And this change must be endured simply because truth beckons.

Thus the fourfold analysis of the world as reality is now complete. In contrast to the 'world as actual', the 'world as real' must be (1) historical; (2) a home, where we belong; (3) a tribunal, where we matter; and (4) a beckoning, in which we submit to the lure. These four dimensions of reality correspond to the four modalities of the inquirer: (1) acceptance (of fate); (2) affirmation (of pleasure); (3) acknowledgment (of guilt); and (4) submission (to beauty). With both the *world* and the *inquirer* now interpreted in this isomorphic correspondence, the phenomenon of truth has been established.

But these analyses demand further questioning. Is there no authority in the quest for truth? That is, in what way, if any, is the search for essences or meaning guided by our reason? Will *any* account suffice? In what way can we determine that our confrontation with an essence is not merely an illusion? In short, even if we accept the account of truth summarized in the previous paragraph, we now must ask the philosophical question—*why?* What *reasons* are there? Indeed, how does *reason* play any role whatsoever in the search for truth?

PART FIVE:
TRUTH AND THOUGHT

13
Truth and Reason

TOUCHSTONE: *Hast any philosophy in thee, shepherd?*
CORIN: *No more but that I know the more one sickens the worse at ease*
he is; and that he that wants money, means and content, is without
three good friends; that the property of rain is to wet, and fire to burn;
that good pasture makes fat sheep, and that a great cause of the night
is lack of the sun; that he that hath learned no wit by nature nor art
may complain of good breeding, or comes of a very dull kindred.
TOUCHSTONE: *Such a one is a natural philosopher.*

Shakespeare, *As You Like It*, III.2

Even the charming if simple shepherd Corin knows what it is to be a philosopher: one who gives and demands reasons. When the motley fool, Touchstone, assures Corin that he is damned, the shepherd demands: "For not being at court? Your reason!" Granted that the reasons given in this wondrous comedy are often fool's reasons, there can be no doubt that this scene is the playful testing and teasing of the philosopher. From the most ancient times philosophy has been recognized as the reason-giving discipline. Indeed, for the philosophers, reason is almost equal to truth itself in importance; the two of them are like partners in a marriage, the lovely bride, truth, sought and wooed by the virile groom, reason. It is their union that promises to be fruitful; alone neither has progeny.

But if truth is the confrontation of essence, how can reason play a role in it? Surely there are no a priori rules or purely formal procedures which can guarantee the proper isolation of an essence. Yet to deny that reason plays any role at all in the essentialist searches of a Plato, a Schopenhauer, or a Heidegger seems an extravagant limitation. There is an *authority* to reason—that is, when reasons are given or when reasoning is applied, we are required to give due consideration or assent. Of course, as Brutus says to Cassius, "good reasons must, of force, give way to better," which suggests that not all reasons are equal. But even reasoning which may not be absolutely compelling still demands our respect, and unless the argumentation is countered, one should yield to its persuasive authority.

It is because reasoning does have this authority that the examiner of reason itself must beware of two obvious dangers. On the one hand, the thinker does not want to restrict reason to purely formal calculi or decision procedures such as symbolic logic, for that would make reason such a rare thing as to be inapplicable to any human circumstance. On the other hand, reason should not be so unrestricted and broadly applied that it loses all authority. Thus, the range and meaning of reason itself become open to question. It becomes clear that the true nature of reason is not as clear as reason would want it to be.

How does one go about the task of defining and describing reason? And how does one judge the extent of its authority, without involving oneself in circularity? Two approaches suggest themselves. One is to note what great philosophers have said about reason, the other is to note and observe the use of reason in certain varied instances. It is not the intent or even the proper task of this inquiry to carry out a complete survey of all possible uses; we are rather concerned solely with the question of how reason applies to the confrontation of truth, so that the isolation of essence is not an ungoverned and random assignment of "sensitive insights." Truth itself is respected just because it is not wanton like opinion; reason likewise is honored because it is not arbitrary.

But what is it that makes reason nonarbitrary? If Corin claims that "a great cause" of the night is the lack of the sun, he is asserting that no other account is as adequate; this is how we *must* think about the cause of night. That, we say, is just exactly what we *mean* by reason. And so, following this insight, Kant defines reason as "the faculty of rules." At times he prefers the metaphor of legislation, describing reason as our source of lawlikeness. In either case, Kant isolates the necessity of lawlikeness from its content, making reason a purely formal faculty which assures us of necessity simply because it lays down principles which cannot be denied.

Reason as Unifier

Kant's account at first glance seems a minimalist description, which is persuasive because of its lean rigor. Certainly we do seem to need rules and laws if there is to be any rational persuasion to our arguments, and if we actually have and use these rules, then they must come from somewhere, so why not simply label the *source* of such regulation reason? Besides, Kant's description does seem to account for the way we actually use reasoning. To reason is to appeal to the laws of thought. What could be simpler?

But Kant is not simple, nor is his account as minimalist as it may at first seem. To reason, according to Kant, is to think in a particular way, that is, according to rules. But to think is to unify. When Corin says the property of rain is to wet, he unifies the concept or term 'rain' with the second concept or term 'wet'. Thus, the unificatory process of thinking is carried out as a unifying law (cause). So it is not only lawlikeness that describes reason, but lawlike unification. At times, Kant identifies this unification as *synthesis:* bringing together.

The supreme bringing together, of course, is that which makes one out of many, just as governmental laws and cultural traditions make *a people* out of many people. To make all into one is to unify the diverse, or to universalize—that is, extend throughout the universe. Universality thus becomes the same as lawlikeness, and hence what is universal is understood not as that which is *accepted* throughout the universe but as that which *must be accepted* throughout the universe. We do not merely agree that "good pasture makes fat sheep," we *must* assent to this claim.

The notion of 'obtaining throughout the universe'—universality—is not limited to the laws which govern the connection of pure concepts (as in logic) or the principles that connect events (as in science), but applies equally well in Kant's moral thinking. For a judgment to qualify as morally obligatory, it must 'obtain throughout the universe'—that is, it must be universalizable. Since I cannot will the breaking of a promise to be a universal law, neither can I accept it as a rule of conduct, and so it is deemed immoral to break a promise. It is not inconsistent with his character for Shakespeare's Corin to add, shortly after the above passage: "I earn that I eat, get that I wear, owe no man hate, envy no man's happiness, glad of other men's good, content with my harm"; and he takes joy in his work. Thus the shepherd not only talks like a philosopher, he acts like one, justifying Touchstone's assessment that he is a "natural philosopher"—a phrase which, in the play, has a wonderfully wicked ambiguity.

To universalize is to achieve authority throughout the universe by unifying under a common rule. Such unity, and consequently such authority, can be accomplished only by the power of reason; or to put the point in other terms, to 'make as one'—to prescribe for all minds—is to reason. How can this power apply to the confrontation of truth in the penetration to essential meaning?

We notice many qualities and characteristics of mothers: they care for their young, they protect and defend them, they teach them most of the important things, how to talk and eat and wash themselves. This list could go on indefinitely. But when we seek to unify all of these characteristics under a single, inclusive notion such as maternal affection, we are merely establishing a general or covering term. However, when we seek to penetrate to the reason which underlies this abstract term 'maternal affection' and focus on the notion of boundless forgiveness grounded in the self-identity of mother with child (if this is indeed the proper essence), the various elements are not merely covered as by an umbrella (the 'general term') but coalesced and hence illuminated by a force which unifies, as a nation unifies many citizens into one people, and synthesized by the power of law. That is, we understand the many elements as manifestations of the essence, *not* merely as members of a class. The isolation of the essence through the power of thought (reason) is the unification or assemblage of the various predicates which make up our multifarious ways of understanding the notion. To penetrate to the essential meaning is to synthesize or unify, and only reason can perform such an act. Thus, by unpacking the Kantian account of reason as the supreme lawgiver of the mind, it is possible to show how such an interpretation admirably fits the confrontation of truth. Reason is therefore not restricted to the mere gathering of evidence or justifications for beliefs that a certain claim is true; rather its greater service is to the unfolding of essential meaning in the phenomenon of truth. It must be stressed that in the uncovering of an essence, what is revealed is not a mere covering term or 'broadest possible class', but an actual, concrete way of existing or thinking which, through its *power*, actually illuminates the various predicates, making them understandable.

Reason as Ideality

For Plato, reason is a dialectic series of regressive steps backward to the fundamental source of intelligibility, which he called the forms or ideas. To think, therefore, is to reach back to the fundamental light which illuminates our everyday world. Plato's forms are probably the most familiar of all classical metaphysical accounts, and may be the most misunderstood. It is not necessary here to interpret the forms, for our interest is not in the ontological principles but simply in what Plato means by thinking or reasoning in what he calls dialectic.

We do idealize. We idealize perfect circles and absolute cold and just states and frictionless machines and perfect vacuums; we idealize every time we rank or judge or assess or seek to understand the meaning of anything. Idealization is one of the ways we think, and under certain conditions such idealizing thinking brings with it an authority not unlike the synthesizing under rules described by Kant. Incredibly, there are some critics who use the term 'ideality' as an indictment, suggesting that whatever is idealized is by its very nature unreal, and hence at most is a mere emotive hope, certainly not something worthy of being called thoughtful or reasonable. But these critics entirely miss the point. Ideality is not utopian.

Suppose I desire to understand what it means to speak. It is possible, of course, simply to observe someone speaking, or even to speak myself and observe how I do it. Let us focus on this latter method. I can bracket as irrelevant the need to account for the history of the English language and even the personal history of how I learned to speak. Nevertheless, even as I write this sentence I realize that there are rules of grammar and syntax which must be utilized if I am to succeed. But success, even if minimally understood as the achievement of mere basic coherence, admits of degrees. Some speakers are more successful than others. Thus the question of how I speak becomes the question of how *well* I speak. Since speaking is necessarily something at which one can relatively succeed or relatively fail, the very intelligibility of speaking includes within it the notion of degrees of excellence. This is even more obvious with other examples: can I even understand the concept of 'running' without the realization that some run more quickly than others, or that running is faster than walking? But speaking is not unlike running: some do it better than others.

How, then, am I to comprehend the meaning of speaking *unless* I include in my understanding the extent to which one speaks well or badly? I recognize that excellence in speech is achieved not merely by adherence to the rules of grammar and syntax, but also by attention to the elements of style. To this I must add the contribution of poets to what language *means*. A simple couplet from Shakespeare, a phrase from Emily Dickinson, a passage from Churchill, a line from W. H. Auden, all reveal that language does wonderful things, and if I attend to such writers I cannot help noticing that the very range and meaning of the language which I myself speak is far greater and more precious than I might have imagined. How am I to grasp the meaning of it?

One obvious way is to understand language *precisely* as that which is wonderfully done by Shakespeare, adequately done by contemporary historians, terribly done by undergraduates, and defeated and abused by network broadcasters. Just as 'running' is made intelligible by the difference between the fast and the slow, so language is made intelligible by the difference between eloquence and vulgarity. Now if one projects the excellence of a thing to its most perfect instance, one can use that projection as a standard or paradigm by which to render intelligible the various levels of success.

This is precisely what Plato does with justice in the *Republic.* By showing us that we can *rank* various kinds of government according to the extent to which they bring about justice, he shows us that we can, by this ranking, project an image of what a perfectly just state would be like. Once this image is established, it is possible to judge how well any actual state participates in this form, and by this to learn what justice is. Thus by the ranking, the form or standard is revealed, and by this form, the meaning or intelligibility of justice is revealed. There is no separate meaning to unranked justice; rather justice is rendered intelligible (and hence thinkable) solely by being ranked in terms of various kinds of government.

One fascinating aspect of the Platonic account of ideality is the explanation of how one can project from the differences of degree to the ideal form. In the *Symposium* and *Phaedrus* this is accomplished through the passion of *eros.* It is thus erotic ideality that allows the thinker to penetrate through the layers of participation to achieve the form or essence. Reason is thus wedded to passion, and no mere formal or lawlike system of principles is adequate. To think is therefore not only to follow laws, it is also to feel the pull of passion. The artificially severe distinction between "purely" intellectual functions and the more satisfying emotional ones is thereby avoided; for after all, it is not one person who merely calculates and another who merely feels, but a single person who passionately thinks and thoughtfully feels; and although we must, in order to make sense of things, distinguish validity from passion, there is no reason to disjoin these two characteristics of our consciousness in such a radical way. One has to *care* about precision and rigor in order to be precise and rigorous, so even in the adherence to rules and laws a passion of some sort must be presupposed.

There is no difficulty in applying Platonic ideality to the phenomenon of confronting essentialist truth. Doubtless in the inquirer's attempt to isolate an essence, steps are taken based upon the degree of success or failure of a notion. Whatever the essence of language might be, surely I cannot confront it without building into the very definition or thinkability of the term the superiority of Shakespearean language over the language found in television advertising. But what is of paramount importance in this realization is that such ranking—and hence intelligibility—can only be the result of reason. Ideality is necessary for essentialist thinking, and it provides us with a kind of reasoning, so that the search for truth remains a rational, and not a wanton, endeavor.

In describing the Kantian and Platonic accounts of the nature of reason, we should perhaps observe that neither thinker is a 'rationalist'. This is to say that neither Plato nor Kant ever maintains that reason, by itself, can somehow inform us of how the world is. Whether one applies the principles of reason to experience, as Kant suggests, or dialectically ranks the varying degrees of excellence to penetrate back to the original form, the authority and universality of reason is always connected with experience or other possible forms of learning. If reason plays a role in the achieving of essentialist truth—as it surely must—it does not exclude the input of other faculties (to use Kant's language for the moment), nor does it seek to establish independent and purely rational knowledge. Truth must be reasonable, and because of the role reason plays, either as a source of rules and universality or as a dialectical regress to a form, it carries with it the force of authority; nevertheless it is not pure formalism or in any way independent of the world. Thus a Cartesian theory or a Leibnizian monadology would not be applicable to the search for essences. There are two reasons why these rationalists are unable to provide a method for confronting essence. The first is the criterion of certainty in their epistemology, the second is their commitment to entities as the basis of their metaphysics.

To confront essential truth is not to identify certain, undoubtable propositions; rather it is to affirm, accept, acknowledge, and submit to reality. In this way, thinking and inquiring—not "knowing for certain"—is possible. The search for essence is the search for that which allows us to succeed or fail in asking and responding, by providing an enclosure in which learning and inquiry can occur. The rationalist's doctrine of epistemic certainty is thus counter to the interests of true philosophy, for the *terminal* nature of certain knowledge renders any further interrogation or asking impossible. Nevertheless, the identification of an essence is by no means a casual or trivial achievement, since it provides the arena in which the continuing awe and wonder of thinking is made intelligible.

Far more serious is the metaphysical presupposition of all rationalism, and that is that entities alone (or 'substances', in seventeenth-century parlance) make up reality. For the seeker of truth in essences, it is not 'the thing' that matters, but meanings. The early rationalists used the term 'essence' to denote the necessary and sufficient conditions for identifying a thing—so that in their methodology, the search was always for a thing's essence, or the essence of an entity. Such metaphysical notions of essence are entirely opposed to the idea of essence developed in the present inquiry, and may well be vulnerable to Wittgensteinian attacks. But the present inquiry concerns itself solely with essential meaning, not things. We do not ask: what *is* language? as if language were a kind of thing or entity; rather we ask: what does it *mean* to speak? We do not ask: what *is* a mother? but rather: what does it *mean* to be a mother? Or, if one cannot identify with the subject in question, one may raise the question: what does it mean for there to be mothers? In any event, the shift is from the language of entities (nouns) to the language of asking what it means for something to be (verbs), and the appeal to reason in such questions therefore is not to causes or conditions necessary to explain *that* something occurs, but to unificatory principles or ways of idealizing. The shift from metaphysical entities to ontological meaning requires a similar shift from reason as a ground for belief that something is true, to reason as a unifying force which makes a notion thinkable—that is, something to affirm or deny, to accept or reject, to acknowledge or refute, to submit to or disdain. Both Plato and Kant have analyzed reason in such a way as to make it applicable to questions of meaning. The claim is made here that not only are there uses of reason which can apply to meaning or essence, but such uses are in fact more fundamental—that is, more rational—than the uses of reason which support a belief in factual claims (knowledge). Being able to *think* (and this means to succeed with authority in the understanding of what something means) is more rational than knowing accurately what is the case. Meaning outranks knowing, and the former is more rational than the latter.

It is of course outrageous to suggest that the great existential ideas of fate, suffering, guilt, pleasure, and ideality, long identified as the proper concern of philosophy and the fundamental thinkers, have no *truth* in them. Indeed, except for a very few academic sceptics, most people consider such issues to be the very meat and marrow of the philosopher's task. What we have seen here, however, is not merely that such ideas have truth, but that they make up a part of the very *meaning* of truth. Thus, it is not enough to reject the narrow assertions of positivism and emotivism; one must succeed in showing the integral part these ideas play in the very possibility of truth. We can think and reason successfully about these ideas only because truth matters; but truth can be shown to matter only by a sufficiently philosophical understanding of these great ideas.

Immanuel Kant has shown what most of us vaguely feel, that pure reason of itself cannot answer the questions about the existence of God, the soul, or freedom—that there is no final solution available to the rational mind that will settle by some calculus or decision procedure how to determine these questions. But this in no way denies truth to such questions. They can still be thought about and reasoned about, and indeed successfully. That is, the philosophical inquiries can advance and enrich and further our understanding, and they can do so only because of the truth inherent in such ideas and in the inquiries which seek to illuminate them and make them worthy of our deepest analysis. It is not necessary that answers to the great questions be known (and hence *settled*) in order for them to be true, nor need they be reduced to mere beliefs or acts of faith or leaps of religion. Reason plays a fundamental role in uncovering or unfolding their truth. Thus we are not left with mere emotion, nor are we abandoned to a critical scepticism toward these majestic ideas.

With the development of this notion of truth, with its emphasis on meaning rather than fact, the life of the mind becomes independent of psychological attitudes, and such achievements as the history of ideas, the cultural reality of a developing people, and poetry and religion are seen as resources for understanding truth. There can be no significant "life of the mind" unless it is grounded in truth, and this inquiry has shown how this is possible. Most thinkers have assumed this to be so, but the presupposition has, for the most part, been left unexamined, or at best merely hinted at; but with this critical examination of what *we* must be like in order to inquire—affirming pleasure, accepting fate, acknowledging guilt, and yielding to seductive beauty—along with an understanding of what the *world* must be like in order to be examined as the source of reality unfolding truth—unfolding as history, providing a dwelling place, functioning as a tribunal, and provoking thought through seduction—an entirely coherent and existentially significant understanding of what truth means has been accomplished. We have always been able to *think* about such matters, but now such thinking is grounded in an account which shows how such thinking is possible.

Imagine, for the sake of concretizing this inquiry, a fanciful primitive society. A small community has been living in a loose but decisive coherence under the inexplicit authority of a powerful chief whose physical strength and aggressive demeanor has bound it together. One day a member of the group takes a pelt that was in the possession of another. We cannot say the first actually *owned* the pelt, since 'ownership' may be an overly sophisticated concept. The strong leader strikes the thief dead with a single powerful blow of his crude weapon. A few days later, a second "thief"—if we can use such advanced terminology to designate the usurper—is similarly dispatched. And then a third is likewise struck down. A few nights later, as the simple ur-society huddles around a fire, an old man, in fairly primitive language, refers to these events. He says first that each of the three former members of the group were killed by the leader because they took a pelt which was not theirs. The group slowly, but decisively, absorbs this fact. Then the old man manages to convey his approval, saying, in effect, that all who so act will be treated in a like manner. The truth of this also sinks in on the group, as new concepts dawn. Finally, the old man says they should have been killed. It was right. Because, he says, this is who we are. The group becomes a reality; a new kind of thinking takes place, a new kind of truth happens.

The crucial point is this: the old wise man, who somehow sees the meaning of what will later be called the *law* literally emerge for the first time in the group's existence, has, in pointing out the meaning of the chief's killing the three usurpers, achieved something far, far greater than anything the chief, by his physical strength, did. For in explaining the acts in this way, he unfolds a profound truth, a truth that changes forever who they are. It is the appreciation of this greatness, the greatness of truth, that marks the tremendous achievement of the mind. It is not the mere action which prompts fear and obedience that matters, it is the quiet but courageous wisdom that tells us how to think about it that matters fundamentally.

Of course, the story is fanciful. It has collapsed into a few days what may have taken centuries, and there is simply no way such a primitive people could discover such power of language in such a simple way. But the story is told to reveal a point of supreme importance. The isolation of the concept 'law', however it is said, is a milestone in the history of truth. It is an event in the life of the mind. But it does not refer to the strong man's acts; rather, the leader's actions actually refer to the old wise man's words. This is the essential meaning of truth. It establishes a kind of pleasure not known before; it tells a story, giving the people a fate which oddly makes them free; it provides a tribunal by which what they do matters, and so they can acknowledge who they are. And it is loved, for it reveals a beauty, allowing them to see, perhaps for the first time. It is fitting that an entirely fanciful story should reveal to us the true worth of truth.

14
Truth and Unity

The dog, struck by a car, lies yapping pitifully on the highway, its back broken. Death would be merciful, but the organism continues to function. It is senseless, unendurable torment, serving no purpose.

The radiant girl, with vibrant youth and stunning beauty, plays the Beethoven violin sonata with such bold energy and yet exquisite touch that all who hear are moved to a rapture of joyous confusion, whether to yield to her feminine loveliness, her brilliant performance, or Beethoven's genius.

The youth, in a gesture of malefic spite and jealousy, knocked over the ink bottle, spreading ruin and envy over the brilliantly drafted drawing. It was mean and petty and small and vicious. But they deemed it an accident.

The television camera, from the earth-orbiting satellite, scans the small, blue planet, on which we, four billion tiny specks, procreating and dying, pollute the globe and pass on meaninglessly into forgotten history.

The youth lived, breathed, dreamed, and waked solely for art. Everything he saw he wanted to paint; his soul thrilled to line, color, space, form, and measure. Even his most casual acquaintances admitted that he belonged in the world of canvas and pigment; here alone was he happy. But his paintings were dreadful. He was overcome with the love and the longing, but lacked all talent.

We can think about each of these images separately and make sense of them. We have our categories and our distinctions. We separate and distinguish, and consequently are not disturbed that one image glorifies, the other reduces to dust. Each image is thinkable in its own terms, illuminated by its own lights. They must be kept separate in order to be thought about. If the distinctions, like chain-link fences, are breached, the images pour out like unleashed beasts, destroying one another in a bedlam of mayhem and riot. We can think about anything, it seems, as long as it is enclosed by the proper limits.

But can we think these images together? Is it not the supreme expectation of the wise that petty meanness and triumphant glory should somehow be brought together in one world? If each idea has its own cocoon, how can the colony survive? But do these images even belong to the same universe? Are people who play sonatas of the same species as those who spitefully ruin a drawing?

In the previous chapter we saw that philosophy, as a reasoned endeavor, seeks unity. It thus becomes imperative to recognize that the truth-seeker is also the unity-seeker. It becomes obvious that the world of yapping dogs with crushed spines is the same world as that of the finest and loveliest art, and that merely to make distinctions is only the first half of thought; the second, perhaps more difficult half is to reunify that which the distinctions divorced to make manageable.

Medieval thinkers would rank the One as among the three great transcendentals, together with the True and the Good. Modern critics look back at this with puzzlement. Why is 'the One' so important? What does it even *mean*, that it can be equated with such lofty notions as the True and the Good? In ancient Greek thinking, Parmenides is noted for his remarkable metaphysics which reduced all to One—a move perhaps admired by scholars from a great distance but totally uncongenial to our present instincts. We know that apples are not oranges, and assume Parmenides must have been dazzled by an error in logic. Today perhaps such terms as 'world' or 'universe' approximate this unifying principle, but these terms entirely lack the energy and vigor of the previous ages. The image of the earth from a satellite may unify us on the blue planet, but it reduces us to tiny replaceable specks. That one of these specks may be a Newton, a Shakespeare, a Rembrandt, is not discernible to the satellite, nor is it within the range of its parameters to render such a judgment possible.

Yet, as the witness swears to tell the whole truth, the philosopher is required to seek the truth of the whole. This truth cannot be the mere abstract one achieved by adding on the reminder that all the images really are a part of one world. For we do not want to know that saints and sinners live on the same block—we know that—rather we want to know how to think about them in terms of each other, for the limits of each image threaten to become the limits of any intelligibility whatsoever, and once we lose the capacity to think these images together we lose the capacity to think at all.

Our earlier discovery that truth is of essences may thus be misleading. For it suggests that truth is a plurality of separate and disjoined essences, each of which can be 'thought' with a total disregard of the others. But we do not want merely to understand the essence of a mother *and* the essence of language, we want to understand what it means to speak as a child of a mother. Unity is a demand of reasoned truth.

Why then is the history of philosophy one vast series of ever more refined distinctions? We pay people professors' salaries to draw distinctions so fine that only graduate students can appreciate their subtleties. We distinguish material from formal implication, *de re* from *de dicto* necessity, equivalence from equality, legality from justice, the sublime from the beautiful, the true from the truth. Every time a philosopher gets backed into a corner by critical argumentation, he makes a new distinction. The webs spread out on finer and finer threads, spinning out further and further from the center until the very intricacy becomes as puzzling as the problem the original distinction was made to solve.

Distinctions, of course, are not just made up. They are discoveries of reason, and without them all thought would come to an end. The danger lies not in making distinctions, but in failing to account for their dual function. For a reasoned distinction serves not only to separate, but to conjoin. Human acts, undistinguished, are not meaningful; but when we distinguish the good from the bad, the acts of men become *conduct,* and hence morally significant. The mistake would be to assume that the distinction between good and bad somehow removes the latter from the realm of the intelligible. To be able to think about acts as moral is to unify them under the coalescing principle of morality; the division between good acts and bad acts does not separate acts from nonacts, but provides a single, unifying principle with which to think about acts as meaningful. To distinguish love from lust does not render the two notions incompatible, but rather shows us how to think about both, for love need not be entirely lust-free, nor lust loveless; the distinction makes a loving lust and a lustful love possible.

We make distinctions to avoid contradictions; we seek the unity in a distinction to achieve coherence. We must make a distinction between body and mind in order to be able to think successfully about who we are. But if we press the distinction beyond its limits, and disjoin body and mind as two distinct metaphysical entities, the difference no longer assists our thinking but impedes it. Descartes is correct in noting the difference; he is incorrect in rendering the distinction beyond all possible unity.

The most dangerous distinction may also be the most necessary. We must note the difference between appearance and reality, yet this distinction seems to seduce all lesser thinkers to a reductionism, in which 'appearance' is seen as mere 'illusion'. Because I can "reduce" Abraham Lincoln to his molecules and atoms, it is claimed that Lincoln "really" is nothing else. Everything beyond these primary bits of matter is mere appearance. The foolishness of such a judgment is insufficient to deter the grim insistence: we must distinguish what is real from how the reality manifests itself. But this is bad metaphysics—and most metaphysics is bad metaphysics—and with such poor reasoning, no truth is possible.

But if we need all of these refined and metaphysically dangerous distinctions, and yet also insist on a unity, how are we to achieve any success? Obviously the passion for distinction must be tempered, and the hunger for unity must be measured, but these are but pious adages unless we know how to temper and to measure. The distinctions must be made with such care that in distinguishing they reveal the underlying unity.

The five images listed at the heading of this chapter are not merely random examples. They were chosen for the purpose of this analysis. Consider the first image. On the one hand our instincts as sensitive and caring beings are offended by the depiction of the unnecessary and terrible suffering of an innocent animal. Yet the description includes the simple clause "but the organism continues to function." And of course, there is the rub. To have dogs at all we must affirm the natural functioning of the organism. We do not *blame* the organism for continuing to function even when all observers, and perhaps even the dog, desperately would wish it to cease. So our anguish becomes a mere subjective, perhaps even romantic and sentimental, indulgence. The organism is supposed to function that way, and if the dog is in pain, so what? And yet, to think this way is to embrace a huge insensitivity, and so we make a distinction. We distinguish 'ought' from 'is', and in so doing ease the mental anguish by relieving ourselves of a contradiction. The dog is suffering (the organism continues to function): we can affirm that as a fact. The dog ought not to suffer: we can affirm that as a moral or pseudomoral judgment. Since morality is separate from metaphysics or science, we do not contradict. Intellectually we heave a sigh of relief; once more the tactic of distinguishing entire systems of thought has saved the mind.

But such relief is illusory. It is precisely because we *can* think of both without contradiction that we seek to understand how they belong together in the same world of meaning. A tension is created by two true judgments: it is, but it ought not be. We think that a young man who loves to paint ought to do so; but if his artistry is bad, we wonder. Nasty people who spill ink on fine drawings out of meanness or spite do exist, but so do great musicians and beautiful people. These judgments also create tension, and the very tension is not eased but exacerbated by the distinctions which render them noncontradictory. If they were contradictory one would be false, and we could dismiss it. But since both can be true, their differences plague the mind with equal demands for acceptance.

How, then, do we think these various images together? What unifies them without destroying their uniqueness or their difference? And how can their appalling differences be rendered compatible? We are outraged by the petty meanness of the ink-spiller, aghast at the unnecessary suffering of the dog, delighted by the violinist, stunned by our smallness and our greatness. But most of all we are overwhelmed that our existence is assaulted by such diverse demands on our thinking. The temptation is simply to distinguish and walk away; but our deepest anguish is that such walking away is cowardly self-deceit. We must confront our existence as ample enough to endure them all, the dog who wants to die but cannot, the girl who dreams of playing and can, the vile toad who spills the ink, the boy who wants to paint but cannot. It is our existence which must endure these diverse tractions and bring them together.

Thus it is the meaningfulness of existence which provides the fundamental unity presupposed by all thought. The meaning of existence is both prior to the distinctions and posterior to their formulation. Who I am matters as a condition of the dog's suffering mattering or the greatness of the violin sonata mattering. I matter just because these are paradoxical modes of existence. Were I not both body and soul I would not be who I am — and if this body wars against the hegemony of this soul, well then the battle is my meaning. For two points must be made: the meaningfulness of existence is the only notion wide enough, ample enough, vast enough, to enclose all the diverse and conflicting modalities which spread out before me like an endless desert. And second, such diverse modalities in turn become the sole resource for the intelligibility of the question about the meaning of my existence. The very paradox and vastness entailed in these differences is how I think about the unity. This is what it means to think.

So how does this work? Truth, we say, is of essences, yet truth also must seek the essential unity of existence. To seek the essence of a mother is to ask: what does it mean to be a mother? This, however, presupposes the greater question: what does it mean to be *at all?* But I learn what it means to be at all by understanding what it means to be a son, a father, a speaker, a moral agent, an artistic observer, a philosopher. What it means to be at all is revealed in being a father or a son; to reveal what it means to be a son is to frame the question in terms of what it means to be at all. The unity of essential being is illuminated by the diversity of essences; the different essential ways of being are in truth only when they are framed in terms of the ultimate unification: being.

This is not as obfuscated as it may seem. The terms 'daughter' and 'father' are possible only because of the more fundamental term 'family' —yet, the family is impossible without the family members. This is synthesis and analysis, and reflection reveals that synthesis is more fundamental. A proper understanding (that is, the truth) of an essence is achieved only when it is seen in terms of its uniqueness (what makes it peculiar), but its uniqueness is possible only because of where and how it fits into the ultimate picture: what it means to be at all. Because among the various ways in which I exist are ways which conflict, the dynamic tension created by accepting these opposing modalities provides illumination by which the whole can be seen. If there were no tensions, there would be no passion to think, and in the absence of such passionate thinking, there would be no meaning. Thus, the unity provided by truth cannot be a resolution or defusing of the tension, but can only be a celebration of it. Truth is an active, not a passive, phenomenon. It is, after all, an active unfolding of the unifying story, the tension between home and tribunal, between yielding to and resisting the allure. Reason must make distinctions because, paradoxically, distinctions make unity possible.

If the 'ultimate picture' which provides the fundamental unity for thought and truth is the meaning of existence, then any way of thinking which distracts us from this integrity is a threat. It does not take a genius to recognize that the variety of misological persuasions which surround the cultural body like a disease function by separating and alienating the multitude of human interests from any centralized focus. We can always see the trees, but not the forest. The danger to any philosophy, or any society for that matter, is always separation, isolation, and alienation. It is an essential part of this inquiry, then, to consider the intellectual forces of disunity. If the above reflections are correct, two major principles must be kept in mind: (1) reason and truth must be harmonized, though not identified; (2) the ultimate harmony or unity is provided only by the meaningfulness of existence. Nihilism, then, is the supreme danger for both truth and reason, since in denying any meaning to existence the nihilist ultimately sunders any connection between the two.

But how are we to understand this nihilistic separation? Consider Plato's comic dialogue *Euthydemus,* in which reasoning is sundered from any concern for truth. The infamous tag team of brothers dazzles its audience, particularly the young and vulnerable for whom Socrates shows protectivist concern, with clever and cunning arguments that seem to show the wise are really stupid and the honorable dishonorable. Who would not be persuaded by these antics of the carnival, which use the somber dictates of reason to make us laugh at the reasoner? Socratic humor may save the reader in this case, but the underlying contagion is still sinister, and Socrates knows it. Today the descendants of Euthydemus continue to dazzle us by having so much fun with uncoupled concepts, creating a playground of intellectualism, where ideas float like bubbles and pop when touched. They foist these unanchored concepts on us in various ways—"conceptual art," for one, in which works can be appreciated merely by being described, and hence need not be seen at all; deconstructionism in both literature and philosophy, for another, where reading becomes a source of self-expression rather than learning or ennoblement; indeed any and all disciplines where the "new" outranks the true, or the zany and bizarre is confused with originality. Reason unlinked to truth is but silliness, the dreaded kind of silliness which is a fecund cancer of the spirit, not because it makes us laugh—for great comic art can achieve this as well—but because it debases all seriousness whatsoever. Plato, and comic artists, may indeed take the playful seriously, but they never make the serious playful.

But if reason without truth is foolish, then truth without reason is terror. For unreasoned truth is simply bigotry. A bigot need not always be false in his judgment: one is a bigot when one adheres to a belief without due cause or justification. Whether in philosophy or in statecraft, bigotry is totalitarian. Terrorism on behalf of an ideology—even if the ideology contains some truth and is inspired, as it often is, by legitimate outrage against social ills—is fundamentally destructive because it is unaccompanied by the checks of thought and support of reason. It is inevitable once one surrenders the need to conjoin critical reasoning with what is believed to be true. To appeal to truth in itself without the *approach* to truth (reason) is to regress back into darkness. It is for this reason that truth, in earlier chapters, was described as an arrest that encloses, not one that terminates. Once again the supreme commitment is to the integrity of the truth-seeker, not the establishment of an orthodoxy.

Less frightening, but no less fatal, is the separation of truth from reason through an appeal to the irrational as a source of benign mystery. It is appalling how many persuaders espouse contempt for reason on behalf of privileged access to secret, mystical, or artistic illumination. "There is more to heaven and earth than is dreamt of in your philosophy, Horatio." Hamlet's remark is so often quoted against the philosopher that one might almost think Shakespeare was an early deconstructionist. Horatio may well have been a rather dull, if loyal, spirit; but philosophy itself has never denied the rich variety of resources for the understanding, it has merely insisted that reasoned evaluation of such resources is more truthworthy than frenzied and uncritical acceptance. Perhaps ghosts do return to urge their sons to revenge, but even Hamlet insists on testing with his own reason the truth of the ghosts' claim.

Let the ghosts tell us what they will, as long as we are willing to listen with both an open *and* a critical ear. Truth without reason is not some privileged access, it is simply dictatorial stupidity. That it abounds where most it is denied with only lip service is by no means surprising.

Metaphysical speculation with no regard for truth or reason—or rather, an *equating* of truth and reason with the sheer pleasure of speculating—is a form of intellectual egalitarianism, which is inevitable once the seriousness and urgency of truth and reason are denied. There are those who would build up 'systems' on weekends, or playfully hop from creed to creed, or seriously urge us to accept a pluralism of doctrines on the plea of tolerance. "All religions are good," they say, and perhaps they are right, but it does not follow that all are *true*. That this last does not *matter* to them is a sign of spiritual prostitution. They want the fun of the thing and are willing to pay for it. Nothing debases like egalitarianism or indifferentism; she may get paid, and he may get laid, but there is nothing worth remembering about it except the minor shame.

On the other hand, an *overly* intimate relationship between the truth and the reasons allowed to support it can be found in almost all closed systems. This type of thinking finds the truth in the system and the system determining the reasons for it. In its negative form, it denies any openness or adventure to the mind; in its most blatant positive form it is merely an elaborate *petitio principii*. Karl Popper has pointed out that systems which include both their own reasons and their own truth cannot be falsified. He mentions Freudian psychology and Marxist political theory as two systems which admit of no falsification. This is bad enough, but such thinking deserves a deeper censure because it produces an inevitable misology. One learns, in the use of such thinking, to hate both truth and reason.

It was noted in Chapter 1 that the false has a thousand names, the truth but one. Perhaps 'thousand' is a hyperbole—it usually is, to no one's dismay—but our reflection on the various ways in which the union between reason and truth may go astray has opened up the seriousness of this final concern. How do we understand the false? Or rather—if we wish to retain the distinction between the true and truth, and therefore restrict the false to propositions or beliefs—how do we understand untruth?

Do you seek the untruth? It is ubiquitous. We see it all around us. The above paragraphs have provided examples sufficient to show us how prolific untruth is. But what is its essence?

We do not equate untruth with error, or even with ignorance. We are finite, and with this realization we must and can endure our limits. Making errors or being ignorant is a part of who we are, and can be incorporated into our reasoning and our love for truth. What we fear, however, is not our ignorance but our being misled; not our errors of judgment but our deception, especially self-deception. This is one of the grounds for our appeal to reason. When the Duke suggests Isabella may be mad, she says:

> O gracious duke!
> Harp not on that; nor do not banish reason
> For inequality; but let your reason serve
> To make the truth appear where it seems hid,
> And hide the False seems true.
>
> *Measure for Measure,* V.1

"Let your reason serve to make the truth appear." In this appeal, Isabella is not merely saying that reasons support our claims to believe, but that *being* reasonable (that is, not being mad) is essential for truth to happen. For untruth is like madness; it is a way of *being* irrational. Untruth is not what is false, but *being* in a false way. It is nihilism. For to disregard the worth of truth is to say that truth does not matter, and to say that is to deny meaning. And so the variant ways we can deceive ourselves about who we are become important resources for understanding both truth and untruth. Nihilism rejects not only truth but reason as well, and so showing how truth and reason belong together is essential for this inquiry.

At the beginning of this chapter five images were presented. For the most part they were rather ordinary kinds of phenomena which occur frequently enough in our everyday experience. But listed together they present us with a question: how do these various phenomena fit into a scheme broad enough to provide that unity which is so fundamental for thought and truth? It was noted that each of the images was quite intelligible when considered singly, and this insight forced us to focus critically on the philosophical passion for making distinctions. When it was uncovered that distinctions unify by making seeming conflicts noncontradictory, the dangers as well as the redemption in such diversity were also revealed. There is the improper use of distinctions which simply leaves the world fragmented, and hence without thinkability as a whole. And there is the proper use which recognizes in distinctions the fundamental urge of reason to find a unity. In the case of the five images the only notion broad enough to render them unified was that of existence itself. And so the great unifier is the question of the meaning of existence.

In spite of its formidable opponent, nihilism, truth retains a curious robustness which renders it oddly but remarkably resistant to its enemies. The ways of deviation may outnumber the way of success, but the lure of truth is powerful. When we reflect on the elements which make up the structure of being in truth, there is much to commend it. Pleasure, fate, guilt, and submission to the allure are what make us open to truth; the world's history, dwelling, tribunal, and seduction account for the unfolding of reality which is what truth means; and reason's achievements of unity and ideality show us how. Now that we are instructed in the armament which is ours by the inheritance of great thinkers, the battle with untruth, though formidable and threatening, is by no means hopeless. We simply must understand what it means to confront the truth in order to be able to resist its enemies.

15
Conclusion

Oh, Courage! could you not as well
Select a second place to dwell?
Not only in that golden tree
But in the frightened heart of me?
Tennessee Williams, *Night of the Iguana*

So intimate and ephemeral is courage that it seems of all the human attributes most resistant to successful analysis; yet courage is as palpable and recognizable as hunger. It is at once the most radiant of all the virtues and the most elusive. Every child knows of its cruel redemption, yet every sage is bewildered by its sphinxian opacity. Saint Augustine pleaded with God to give him chastity — but not yet. Who would not plead to have courage delayed indefinitely? For to be courageous is to be in torment. The greater the anguish, the greater the courage, so who could possibly want it in abundance? Who could possibly want it at all?

But what could an understanding of courage possibly contribute to the present inquiry into truth? In this, the final chapter, in which one expects a concluding synthesis or review, why turn the reader's attention to a seemingly new endeavor, an examination of courage, which seems to have little or nothing to do with truth? Since to answer this question is to carry out the analysis, a certain indulgence must be asked of the reader to show that this final topic is indeed fitting for the ultimate synthesis in the attempt to understand truth.

And so we present as the concluding task an attempt to isolate the essence of courage — to penetrate through to the *truth* of courage. But how do we begin? Courage and cowardice, we say, consist in doing or failing to do . . . what? What we ought to do? What is proper? Laches, as we saw earlier, suggested the warrior's image of 'staying at one's post', and we understand by that simply doing one's duty. It is not a bad suggestion, but it raises sufficient problems that it must ultimately be discarded. The primary reason this 'moral account' of courage must be dismissed is that it is backwards. Morality does not explain courage; rather, courage explains morality. The concrete, existential confrontation of one's self is more fundamental than the metaphysical speculative realms of morality, and far more fundamental than mere psychological investigations of 'feelings' of obligation and the 'fear' of consequences. Fear certainly belongs in the phenomenon of courage, but neither fear nor a 'sense' of duty which apparently opposes it can illuminate what it means to be courageous or cowardly. Nor can a purely formal appeal to the abstraction 'choice' render courage intelligible, for choice does not make courage possible, but courage renders choice possible, by making it meaningful.

And yet, it would seem we must assume morality in order for there to be courage. For if one suggests that courage is doing what one *ought* to do in the face of danger, then whatever constitutes the 'ought' must come first, and hence is presupposed. But of course we all know it is possible to be courageous even when there is no moral choice; and further, it may even sometimes be courageous to do that which is immoral. Indeed, one of the greatest tributes to heroes is that in their valor they have gone "above and beyond the call of duty," which suggests a transmoral character to this elusive virtue; for certainly if I am praised for courage in going *beyond* duty it cannot be merely duty, or the adherence to it, that makes me courageous.

Kant has argued that the only absolutely good thing is a good will, which may be completely correct; but he goes on to define a good will as one in complete accord with the moral law. This argument, though brilliant in one way, seems to leave out the most important point. How is this 'accordance' achieved? If, as Kant says, it is due to 'the will', then it is not *being* in accordance which deserves to be called good, but rather the strength or the conviction or the power which *makes* the will good. But if something other than the will makes the will good, then the will's goodness is not absolute, but derived. Furthermore, Kant's definition of the good will as one in accord with the moral law suggests that an untempted, untried, 'naturally good' will is superior to the tempted, anguished, and ultimately triumphant will which has suffered occasional defeat in its attempt to do what is right. The good will is good for a reason, and that reason must *include* the struggles with cowardice and inclination. Kant's brilliant insight is distracted by his insistence on using the language of faculties.

It might be argued that by using the term 'will', Kant expects us to include within the concept the struggles and the tensions between good and bad. And perhaps this expectation is warranted, but Kant does not make it explicit. For the language of 'the will', especially when it is opposed to 'nature' or 'natural inclinations', is the language of metaphysics. There is no sillier argument, as Hume and others have pointed out, than the so-called dispute over free will and determinism. The appeal to faculties may be wonderful in transcendental epistemology, but it is fatal in metaphysics, for 'faculties' inevitably become 'entities', and the prohibition against the reification of abstractions is transgressed. The point that must be made here is simply that neither metaphysical nor moralist language is adequate to explain *why* we do what we ought.

A man who confronts his own fate nobly is 'freer' than one who has maximized his options. The truth of this strikes us and reveals itself in the refinement of what the term 'free' truly means. This is not to espouse some grim fatalism, nor is it to champion the darker side of man by celebrating his chains; it is merely to recognize the autonomy of 'freedom' from any metaphysical presuppositions or psychological dependence on options. But if we cannot gain purchase on metaphysical or psychological tracks, how can we inquire at all into the phenomenon of freedom?

It is not freedom but courage that is fundamental. The confusions result from ranking metaphysical speculation above the concrete, existential analysis of how we exist. And among the fundamental ways we exist are cowardice and courage.

Perhaps by examining the lure of weakness we may discover how to think about these fundamental ways to be. When we are faced by an approaching danger or challenging confrontation, what tempts us to simply avoid the matter by indifference or flight? Surely the most insidious voice that would distract us from our duty and honor is that which tells us we do not really matter. Will the battle really be lost if I, poor quaking soul, leave my post? I am but one among thousands; my absence will not be noted, or at least will not matter. Confess to my friend my petty treachery? Is the friendship worth that much pain? Am I worthy of the friendship? If I belittle my own importance there is no need to confront my failings. Self-abnegation or false humility is the coward's greatest balm, for under the guise of misprized modesty we can avoid all need of any courage whatsoever. What does it matter if we fail? Is not our nature so flawed and so impecunious that it were but conceit and arrogance to pretend we matter to the extent that the fearsome anguish of confrontation is even expected of us? The easiest way to tempt ourselves, as we all know too well, is to debase our own importance. Why endure the pain if we matter so little?

If we accept this account of why we might yield to cowardice, is there anything in the depiction which points to the essential truth of courage? If what tempts us away from courage is the debasing of our own worth, perhaps courage is the acceptance or the embracing of our own worth. To be courageous, then, is to recognize that we do matter, that we have worth simply in being who we are, and that whatever actions we might take deserve to follow from the bold confrontation of our own being. This is the implicit suggestion of our analysis of the coward. Are there any other hints?

In Shakespeare's play, when King Richard II begins to sink into despair, his companion makes a telling appeal:

> AUMERLE: Comfort, my liege. Remember who you are!
> KING RICHARD: I have forgot myself. Am I not king?
> Awake thou sluggard majesty, thou sleepest!
> *Richard II,* III.2

Merely by recalling to mind who he is, Richard is able to infuse a sense of nobility into his plight. This is no mere random quotation; the whole tragedy of *Richard II* is about Richard's confrontation of and retreat from his own worth. Those whose curious task it is to infuse into the young the daring to endure unspeakable hardships almost always do so by attempting to awaken in the recruits a sense of their own importance, often by appealing to their inheritance and patriotism.

Consider the prayerful supplication of Williams's poem that banners this chapter. Why does the poet plea for courage? As we have seen, to ask for courage is to ask for torment, so why would a frightened man ask for courage? The coward is one whose continued untroubled existence is preferred to a meaningful, though troubled, one. The poet knows that to be cowardly is to shrink, to become small; it is ultimately to be eclipsed; it is not to matter. Shame is loss of significance, a surrender of one's importance and belonging. Unlike simple wrongdoing, shame tastes like rotten fruit or ashes in the mouth—something to be spit out and forgotten. And so, incredibly, we ask for courage, not because we *want to* matter in some posttraumatic state, but because we matter *now.* What we fear is not the pain, but the forgetting. The poet asks for courage as he asks for remembrance, for in forgetting who he is, the poet or the king realizes a loss of meaning.

It is therefore not presumptuous to suggest that to be courageous is to confront the worth of one's own existence, to accept the burden and the honor that who one is matters, that it is important to be. The acts of valor follow from this fundamental, existential confrontation.

But in suggesting this we have rendered courage almost identical to truth. Truth, as we have seen, is the confrontation of reality unfolding our meaning; courage is the confrontation of one's meaning as something that matters. Is there a difference?

Of course, truth and courage are not the same. At present, however, it is their astonishing similarity that compels our attention. But how can two such seemingly diverse notions have such compelling similarity? Before we reject this similarity out of hand, however, it may be well to remind ourselves that no less a thinker than Plato has argued in a similar vein.

In the *Republic,* the class of warriors, whose identificatory virtue is courage, must first be established as separate and autonomous from the class of ordinary citizens, whose membership in the community is based on self-interest. But it is only from this isolated and rarified class of the courageous that one selects the even smaller group who can rule because of their love of truth. Only the courageous can become wise, according to this suggestion, and truth itself becomes available to the thinker only by serious reflection on the warrior. Indeed, at several moments in the discussion, such as in the comparison of the philosopher to a dog, Socrates seems to identify the philosopher with the warrior, as if their difference were merely a matter of degree.

To appeal to Socrates is not an appeal to holy writ, though his reasoning is as impressive as any in the long history of this curious struggle. Of course truth is not courage; the two terms have different and distinct meanings. Socrates knew this, and the present inquiry perforce retains the distinction. But both Socrates and this inquiry attest to the realization that just as rulers are naked without warriors, so truth is vacuous without courage. It is precisely because we already know that the two terms, truth and courage, are different that it is possible to define them in such boldly similar ways. In courage we confront our meaning; in truth we confront reality as the unfolding of meaning, and a part of our being in truth is the courageous enduring of our fate.

Thus both courage and truth rely on confrontation, and so we must ask: what does it mean to confront? It means to come face to face with that from which we would turn away but cannot. We are, in confrontation, both attracted and repelled, drawn to and drawn away from. Confrontation is thus more than merely observing or witnessing, for there can be neutrality in these; but to confront is necessarily to endure the tension between the opposing forces of attraction and repulsion. In courage what repels is the fear of pain, what attracts is the lure of significance and wholeness. The very tension between these two countering forces adds to the anguish, so that it almost seems one needs courage in order to have courage. This is not unlikely, since the poet prays for courage, and in praying he already reveals his being courageous.

Truth, on the other hand, is a confrontation because the unfolding of reality burdens us with fate and guilt, that is, acceptance and acknowledgment. At the same time it attracts us with both pleasure and beauty, that is, affirmation and submission. Thus, as with courage, we do not merely observe or witness truth, but confront it; it is an active and not a passive modality. But it must be emphasized that confrontation requires the facing of a dynamic phenomenon, and hence cannot be understood merely as a formal relationship, nor can its essence be approached in any way other than a concrete, existential one.

Courage is sweat in the palms, a tightening in the groin, a quickening of the pulse, a shortness of breath, a struggle to resist withdrawal. These are all physical, concrete, immediate experiences. Yet it is also a confrontation with meaning, a reasoned analysis of what it means to exist, an establishing of the fundamental possibility of freedom, in which to be free means to be able to be responsible, to be guilty, to *matter.* This concrete isomorphism between the confrontation of essence-grounding truth and the confrontation of freedom-grounding courage is the *philosophical* justification for the curious Christian teaching that "the truth shall make thee free." The truth shall make us free because in confronting essence we reveal the meaningfulness of our existence which entails that we matter; but to matter at all is to be free, and freedom is grounded in courage.

And so, with this, one of the final clinging puzzles about the praise of truth has been, if not exactly answered, at least given a response. There is a connection between truth and freedom: courage. Properly understood, the connection is neither outrageous nor undisciplined romanticism: it makes existential sense.

But even if the 'connection' between truth and freedom makes existential sense, why should this inquiry conclude with an analysis of such a connection? Courage, after all, is not an *element* of truth the way acknowledgment or unfolding is. There may be an impressive isomorphism between being in truth and being courageous, but since truth can be examined adequately without any reference to courage, as this inquiry has shown, the culmination of these investigations with a study of courage must have a more compelling reason.

In order to appreciate the full impact of the need to embrace courage as we complete our investigation of truth, it is necessary to consider a particularly dreadful realization. Many philosophers impart a certain quality or flavor to the entire range of their thinking by pointing out singular questions or disturbing insights which they consider to be central to the symptoms of this fever known as philosophy. For Descartes the question is of the indubitable; for Socrates it is self-knowledge. Nietzsche points to the Eternal Recurrence as his most dreadful doctrine, and Aquinas focuses on questions about analogies to God. Yet there is one question — or it may be formulated as a dread realization — that few if any thinkers have honored by raising, but that seems to me of utmost seriousness and of devastating significance. And it is this question — or dread realization — that accounts for our need for courage.

It may be put first as a question: why does not our ignorance, which is appalling, or our confusion, which is vast, provide us with a refuge? Knowing so little, and beguiled by our own limitations, why are we not excused from the unachievable burden of truth? Stunned with our ineptitude, can we not enter a plea of diminished, or even nugatory, responsibility? If we are indeed finite, how can the infinite burden of truth be weighed against us?

To raise it first as a question, however, is merely to be gentle and hence cruel. It deserves to be presented as the most dreadful realization which the entreating mind must confront: our confusion offers no solace; the beguiled are not thereby forgiven. Ignorance of the law, it is said, is no excuse; but ignorance of truth we think should be, yet we realize, as profoundly as we submit to any certainty, that it does not excuse. What else but icy dread and fatal anxiety can follow from this fell realization? We cannot escape through appeals to native innocence, like children, or like Eve, the full and awesome burden of truth. Though it seems highly unfair, we realize that being in untruth is unlicensed, and so we are burdened with a duty which cannot be fulfilled.

Ignorance usually does excuse. If I am unaware of the harm that will ensue, I cannot be held responsible for doing what brings the harm about. Furthermore, most of us accept Kant's dictum that 'ought' implies 'can'—that one can be obliged to do only that which is possible. I cannot have a moral obligation to cure all who suffer from disease, for I do not know the remedy. Thus it would seem that my enforced ignorance of the great metaphysical questions redeems me from the burden of the impossible. If I cannot know for certain whether God exists, or if he does, what his nature is; if I cannot determine with any degree of assurance whether I have a soul, or a free will, or even a role, purpose, function, or place in the vast measure of reality; if I cannot answer with terminal satisfaction any of the great moral and ethical questions which loom, unenlightened, like a rolling fog—then surely I cannot be expected to struggle with these dark and unyielding foes. Let those who espouse belief offer their responses; but since beliefs are many and the truth but one, there can be no settlement in the conflicts of faith. It would seem we can only allow for belief on grounds other than reason, knowledge, or certainty, and hence it cannot matter if our beliefs are wrong.

But these appeals are bootless. We acknowledge an obligation to truth regardless of these pleas for innocence. I do not know this as I know the rules of geometry or the fact that sugar dissolves in water; but I must affirm it, accept it, acknowledge it, and embrace it. To do this in the face of the grim realization of its enormity and our poverty requires a boldness of spirit equal to the sinister dread of the seeming inevitability of failure. It requires courage. But here the term 'requires' is not an idle one, as if we were to say that courage would be a nice commodity to have. The point is that if we are denied knowledge and certainty, yet at the same time obligated to confront the truth, then courage is a logical necessity. We may not be offered the weapons necessary to win the battle, but we are offered the courage to endure the defeat. Defeat endured, however, is defeat defeated.

This may be called the most dreadful realization confronting our finite minds because it closes off forever the only two exits which would be welcome: the satisfaction of terminal answers, or the retreat to the quietude of indifference. We cannot shrug our shoulders and merely admit to our ignorance. We cannot take refuge in religious leaps that sever us from our own confusion. We cannot even smirk in the arrogance of scepticism. To be sure, many do seek inauthentic refuge in these retreats, but their apparent shelter is deceptive, their solace dishonorable. They are forms of self-deception and hence of self-loathing.

We have already discovered that courage is the fundamental awareness that who we are matters. If indifference, uncritical beliefs, and scepticism all entail self-deception and self-loathing, as they do, then courage is an antidote to these ills. But how is courage a *philosophical* weapon against the greater threat of untruth? If we are not provided with the armor of knowledge, we are at least given the sword, courage. Thus courage, as the confrontation of our own worth, becomes integral both to the method and to the meaning of truth. It is to these two final considerations that we must now briefly turn.

Why this method? Since it is impossible to make metaphysical leaps beyond experience to a direct awareness of ultimate reality, it is obvious that any inquiry into truth or courage must begin from a consideration of our own occurrence within the world. But how am I to raise *this* question? I may ask: what *kind of thing* am I, the analysis of which would reveal how truth and courage are possible? Obviously if I begin such an account with pure physical elements, such as hearts, muscles, nerve endings, and brains, I cannot discover the answer. This is not because such investigations are invalid or because such entities do not exist— they obviously do—rather it is simply the case that the ways we think about such things as muscles and nerve endings are not capable of providing us with the kind of response needed to answer the question.

Suppose, however, we augment the list by including such 'metaphysical' entities as minds, spirits, souls, and wills. These additions may indeed bring us closer to the possibility of making sense of truth and courage, but their very existence as entities is suspect. Furthermore, they seem to provide us answers solely because we design them so as to give us the answers. Thus these attempts turn out either to be circular or to involve unverifiable presuppositions. In other words, the arguments against such entities are no worse and no better than the arguments for them.

And so, we are forced to consider solely the *ways* in which we exist in the world, which are available to us through reflective experience and rational analysis. In this way, our own being courageous and our own confronting of truth is made available to us in the same way that Descartes' own thinking was available to him as the ultimate source of his *Meditations.* And so we simply ask what is involved when we affirm something as true, accept it as true, acknowledge it as true, and submit to it as true. Our ability to reflect on what these modalities mean is perhaps a remarkable capacity, but such reflection doubtless takes place, and there is no reason to assume any metaphysical claims at all in order to undertake it. Mistakes can be made, of course, but they are discoverable as any mistake is unearthed, by criticism of the arguments, by appeal to broader and richer experience, and by testing the capacity of the analyses to throw light on our own thinking. The very fact that mistakes are made and then uncovered reveals the integrity of the enterprise.

Thus the present inquiry has raised the question of truth in terms of the existential phenomena which *arrest* the seeking. There seem to be four. These, of course, can be challenged within the same methodology, and the reader is invited to do so. But the reasoning for such selection together with the analysis of each of the four has provided a meaningful and nonfantastic account. The procedure has also shown the weakness of any theoretical account of truth that does not begin with this fourfold confrontation, and hence its appeal to the reader becomes one of judgment and assessment. If a reader finds it somewhat unusual to inquire into truth by analyzing the existential phenomena of pleasure, fate, guilt, and beauty, he is free to evaluate the analyses and interpretations as critically as he may, but he should not dismiss the entire attempt merely because it is original—though I have tried to show throughout that the claims are more modest, and even to some extent less "original," than may at first seem.

The final suggestion, however, is that courage can be found as illuminating every step of the fourfold analysis of confrontation. This claim gives us the opportunity for a final, conclusive review.

Courage as a mode of truth. There are two fundamental starting points for this analysis of truth: (1) that truth is an answer, or at least a response, to a question, and hence terminates or encloses the interrogation, and (2) that the response of the questioner consists in a confrontation of this arrest, in terms of affirmation, acceptance, acknowledgment, and submission. The inquirer confronts truth, whereas the world (as reality) bestows truth as meaningfulness. There is no need to repeat the arguments for these two starting points. Rather we shall review them here in such a way as to reveal their underlying connection with the virtue of courage.

Truth arrests. That is, truth brings us to a halt; it impedes the ever restless search or hunger for what is sought. This arrest is articulated in terms of the four ways in which we are stopped in our tracks. When confronted with that which permits of no further asking, no further inquisition, investigation, or speculative rumination, what can we do? What *do* we do? When I have reached my goal, I rejoice in it—taking pleasure; when I am required to cease my probings, I accept it—as fate; when I am uncovered as responsible, and hence can hide no longer, I acknowledge it—as guilt; and finally, when I am stunned into speechless awe at the final radiance, I submit to it—as beauty. In each of these cessations, however, there is a confrontation of that beyond which I cannot go, and therefore there is a challenge to my very inquisitorial existence—my role as seeker, as predator, as hunter, as lover is not only stopped, it is, as we have seen, enclosed. This enclosure is a form of self-acceptance; I am confronted with both my limits and my restlessness. In confronting what turns out to be a kind of mirror, I discover myself. But to accept who I am is to arrive at the existential realization that who I am matters. If I do matter, however, I am barred from retreat, I am forced to confront myself, I must admit that not only can I never know for certain the answers to the great metaphysical questions, but my own confrontation itself means that who I am and what I do is no longer irrelevant or insignificant. But this bold acceptance that who I am and what I do *matters* is the essential meaning of courage.

It is courageous to accept my fate. It is courageous to acknowledge my guilt. But it is also courageous to affirm what I am, in the rejoicing of pleasure, and to yield to what is revealed in the submission to its beauty. So the fourfold structure of confrontation reveals the meaning of courage.

Yet, courage is also necessary for a home to matter, for a tribunal to weigh my worth, for my story to unfold with the dread inevitability of my fate. And it is courageous to yield to the allure of the unfolding beauty that is the world as my desire. So courage is found to lie in the very unfolding of truth.

All true philosophical inquiry is both *experiential* (though not necessarily 'empirical') and *reflective*. Working carefully backwards, from the disturbing, tentative reflections on the worth of truth in Chapter 1 and the unsettling paradox of truth in Chapter 3, through the distinction between the true and truth, and the spotting of essence as the proper realm of truth, this inquiry has been guided solely by reflection on and analysis of the notion of truth. We *experience* the term in our language; and this means more than merely to *use* it. We test it in possible combinations, we try out insights, and we learn to avoid the pitfalls of dangerous ideologies, in part by reading and critically reflecting on the prior accounts of truth by great philosophers. We do not shun the magnificent insights of the poets or even the wisdom of religious thinkers. For why should we close off access to *any* resource that seems to throw light on such a difficult problem? None of these resources is accepted without criticism and critique, so why should they be feared? A poet's brilliance, or the insightful devotion of the pious, belongs to our tradition and our inheritance, and thus constitutes a part of our experiential reservoir. What matters is the sense we make of these contributions, not the impeccability of their pedigree. As an inquirer into the meaning of truth, I am willing to learn from any source whatsoever, as long as I can test it, measure it, weigh it, and wonder how it fits into the grand unfolding of the meaning of truth.

And grandeur is, indeed, a fitting, if final, attribute of truth.